I0447481

Highlights of GAO-12-65, a report to congressional requesters.

December 2011

DEATH SERVICES

State Regulation of the Death Care Industry Varies and Officials Have Mixed Views on Need for Further Federal Involvement

Why GAO Did This Study

Media reports have identified instances of desecration of graves and human remains at cemeteries, and in one instance, reported that bodies were removed from graves and the sites resold. Allegations have also surfaced about the mismanagement of pre-need plans that are designed to provide consumers the opportunity to fund funeral and cemetery arrangements before they are needed. The FTC's Funeral Rule requires that, among other things, funeral providers give consumers lists that disclose the cost of funeral goods and services before they enter into funeral transactions. Proposed legislation introduced in March 2011 would increase the federal government's role in regulating the industry by, among other things, requiring that the FTC regulate aspects of cemetery operations. GAO was asked to review the regulation of the death care industry. This report discusses (1) how federal and state governments regulate the industry and how regulation has changed since 2003 and (2) state regulators' views on the need for additional regulation.

GAO reviewed FTC's Funeral Rule and interviewed officials representing the FTC and national industry and consumer associations; surveyed state officials to gather data on state regulation of the death care industry; and, where possible, compared the results of the 2011 surveys with those of similar surveys GAO conducted in 2003. The response rate for our 2011 surveys ranged from 78 to 84 percent. GAO also reviewed laws and regulations. GAO is not making any recommendations in this report.

View GAO-12-65 or key components. For more information, contact William O. Jenkins, Jr. at (202) 512-8777 or jenkinswo@gao.gov. To view the e-supplement online, click on GAO-12-91SP.

What GAO Found

The extent to which the federal and state governments regulate the death care industry—funeral homes, cemeteries, crematories, pre-need funeral plans, and third party sales of funeral goods—varies, as does the extent to which regulation has changed since GAO last reported on the regulation of the death care industry in 2003. The Federal Trade Commission (FTC) continues to annually conduct undercover shopping at various funeral homes to test compliance with the Funeral Rule. Of the over 2,400 funeral homes that the FTC shopped since 1996, the FTC reported an overall compliance rate of about 85 percent. With respect to state regulation, consistent with GAO's findings in 2003, the way in which states regulate the industry varies across industry segments and states. Also, the extent to which state regulators reported that they had specific rules or regulations for each industry segment in both 2003 and 2011 varied. Most consistent across states in both years was reporting that there were specific rules or regulations for funeral homes (94 and 95 percent in 2003 and 2011, respectively). In contrast, 77 percent of state regulators of cemeteries reported that their states had specific rules or regulations for cemeteries in 2003, and 88 percent reported this in 2011. Certain state regulators also reported that their states made various statutory or regulatory changes since 2003, primarily to clarify legislation or regulation or to enhance consumer protections, and that they believe these changes strengthened their regulatory program to varying degrees. State regulators reported that these changes came about for a variety of reasons, including accounts of desecration of human remains or proposals from state agencies and industry groups.

State regulators' views on the need for additional federal and state regulation of the industry varied, as shown in the figure below.

State Regulators' Views on the Need for the Federal and State Governments to Take a More Active Role in Regulating the Death Care Industry, as Reported in 2011

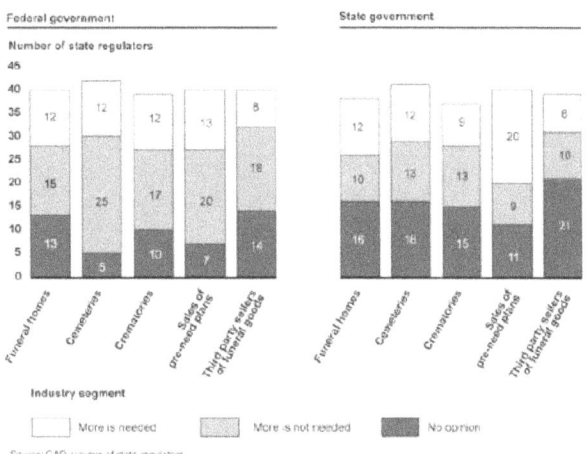

The FTC provided technical comments, which GAO incorporated where appropriate.

_____ **United States Government Accountability Office**

Contents

Tables

Figures

Abbreviations

FTC   Federal Trade Commission

View GAO-12- 91SP key component

DEATH SERVICES: 2011 Surveys of State Regulators (GAO-12-91SP),
an E-supplement to GA0-12-65

United States Government Accountability Office
Washington, DC 20548

December 15, 2011

The Honorable Herb Kohl
Chairman
Special Committee on Aging
United States Senate

The Honorable G.K. Butterfield
Ranking Member
Subcommittee on Commerce, Manufacturing and Trade
Committee on Energy and Commerce
House of Representatives

The Honorable Bobby L. Rush
House of Representatives

In recent years, the media has reported on instances of desecration of graves and human remains at cemeteries and, in at least one instance, reported that at Burr Oak Cemetery in Illinois, bodies were removed from graves and the sites were resold. Concerns have also arisen over the sale and management of pre-need plans—plans that involve the prepayment and prearrangement of funeral and cemetery goods and services to be provided at the time of death—because of allegations of the mishandling of funds.[1] Aside from the Federal Trade Commission's (FTC) Funeral Rule—a rule that affords consumers certain rights when making funeral arrangements, such as requiring funeral providers to provide price lists to consumers—the federal government generally does not regulate the marketing practices of the death care industry, which includes businesses that provide funeral and cemetery goods and services.[2] Recent concerns have inspired a discussion regarding whether the federal government should take a greater role in regulating various segments of the death care industry. For example, federal legislation introduced in March 2011—the Bereaved Consumer's Bill of Rights Act of

---

[1] For more information on pre-need plans and reported incidents regarding these plans, see app. II.

[2] See 16 C.F.R. pt. 453 (codifying the FTC's Trade Regulation Rule on Funeral Industry Practices, commonly referred to as the "Funeral Rule").

2011—would, if enacted, expand the FTC's role in protecting consumers in arranging death care transactions, including services at cemeteries.[3]

The death care industry encompasses (1) funeral homes, (2) cemeteries, (3) crematories, (4) pre-need plans, and (5) third party sales of funeral goods.[4] Our prior work on the death care industry found that most regulation of the industry occurred at the state level and that states varied in their approaches to regulating the death care industry. We reported in both 1999 and 2003 that it is not possible to determine the extent of the problems in the death care industry since accurate data on the number and types of consumer complaints made against the industry were not available.[5] However, in light of recent concerns over instances of wrongdoing and allegations of mismanagement within the industry, you asked us to update our previous work on state and federal regulation. This report follows up on our previous work and discusses (1) how the federal and state governments regulate the death care industry, and how regulation has changed since 2003, and (2) to what extent regulators believe that more regulation is needed.

To address our objectives, we analyzed the FTC's Funeral Rule, as well as proposed federal legislation relevant to the death care industry—the Bereaved Consumer's Bill of Rights Act. We also analyzed FTC documents to gain a better understanding of the Funeral Rule, such as reports on funeral providers' compliance with the Funeral Rule and consumer and industry guides. We also contacted the National Association of Attorneys General to obtain perspectives on states' coordination with the FTC. Further, we reviewed national association documents relevant to the management and regulation of the industry, such as model guidelines and consumer guides. In addition, we interviewed officials from the FTC and six national associations to obtain their views on the level of state and federal regulation, how it has

---

[3] See H.R. 900, 112th Cong. (1st Sess. 2011). A substantially similar bill had been introduced in September 2009. See H.R. 3655, 111th Cong. (2d Sess. 2009).

[4] Third party sellers of funeral goods includes retailers of caskets, urns, monuments, that are not affiliated with a funeral home or cemetery.

[5] GAO, *Funeral-Related Industries: Complaints and State Laws Vary, and FTC Could Better Manage the Funeral Rule*, GAO/GGD-99-156 (Washington, D.C.: Sept. 23, 1999), and *Death Care Industry: Regulation Varies across States and by Industry Segment*, GAO-03-757 (Washington, D.C.: Aug. 25, 2003).

changed, and what more, if anything, is needed.[6] We also surveyed state regulators from all 50 states that have responsibility for regulating or oversight of each of the five death care industry segments to gather information on each state's regulatory efforts and their views on the current level of regulation.[7] To do this, we gathered information from a variety of industry sources to identify state regulators for each the five industry segments in all 50 states, contacted each state regulator to confirm their information, and then distributed a total of 250 surveys—one survey for each of the five industry segments in all 50 states. Our surveys, which were administered from April 2011 through June 2011, were designed to garner responses to many of the same questions we asked in our 2003 survey of state regulators to enable us to determine whether there had been changes in states' approach to regulating the various segments of the industry.[8] We received a response rate of 78 to 84 percent for each of our surveys.[9] Finally, we collected more specific information from state regulatory officials and state industry and consumer association representatives in five states—Colorado, Illinois, Oregon, Tennessee, and Wisconsin. We selected these states based on the results of our preliminary work, including whether legislative or regulatory changes had been made or proposed and whether any major incidents or issues related to the death care industry had occurred in this

[6] We interviewed officials from the following associations: the (1) Cremation Association of North America; (2) Funeral Consumers Alliance; (3) International Cemetery, Cremation, and Funeral Association; (4) International Conference of Funeral Service Examining Boards; (5) North American Death Care Regulators Association; and (6) National Funeral Directors Association. We also contacted the National Association of Insurance Commissioners to obtain information on pre-need insurance plans, but an official from the association stated that it had limited information on the issue because pre-need is not considered a separate line of business from other insurance programs. We selected associations based on referrals from FTC staff and our preliminary discussions with industry officials.

[7] We did not include the District of Columbia in our 2003 survey and, as a result, did not include the District of Columbia in our 2011 survey either since we planned to compare survey responses from both years.

[8] Our surveys primarily asked state regulators to provide current information on the regulation of the industry. However, some questions asked regulators to provide data since 2003, some asked questions for data since 2008, and other questions asked about specific data for each year in 2008, 2009, and 2010.

[9] All but two states—Michigan and New Hampshire—responded to at least one of our five surveys. We did not independently verify the accuracy or completeness of the responses to the surveys. This report does not contain all the results from the surveys. The surveys and a more complete tabulation of the results can be viewed at GAO-12-91SP.

state in recent years. For each of these states, we reviewed relevant documents, such as death care related statutes and regulations, task force and audit reports, and position papers to better understand (1) how their state regulates the industry; (2) what, if any, concerns exist; and (3) how, if at all, requirements have changed. In addition, within these states, we interviewed officials from a total of eight regulatory entities, seven industry-related state associations, two consumer-oriented state associations, and an attorney general's office.[10] Because we used nonprobability sampling to select case study states, the information we obtained from these five states cannot be generalized to all states. However, the case studies provided us with additional information on how states regulate the industry.

We conducted this performance audit from October 2010 to December 2011 in accordance with generally accepted government auditing standards. Those standards require that we plan and perform the audit to obtain sufficient, appropriate evidence to provide a reasonable basis for our findings and conclusions based on our audit objectives. We believe that the evidence obtained provides a reasonable basis for our findings and conclusions based on our audit objectives. Additional details on our survey methodology are contained in appendix I.

Background

Regulatory Roles

Funeral homes, cemeteries, crematories, pre-need plans, and third party sales of funeral goods are all various segments of the death care industry, and the federal and state governments both have a role in regulating the industry. In 1999 and 2003, we reported on various aspects of federal and state regulation of the death care industry.[11] Among other things, we stated that with respect to the federal government's role in regulating the death care industry, aside from the FTC's Funeral Rule, there is no other regulation that specifically addresses the marketing practices of the death care industry at the federal level; most regulatory

---

[10] In each of these states, we selected the regulatory entities that had regulatory responsibilities over the industry. We selected associations based on referrals from state regulators and national associations.

[11] GAO/GGD-99-156 and GAO-03-757.

responsibilities regarding the industry are handled at the state level.[12] The FTC's Funeral Rule, which became fully effective in April 1984, provides, among other things, that consumers are entitled to price information about funeral goods and services before they purchase them, which would enable the consumer to use the information for comparative shopping if he or she wishes. For example, the Rule declares it an unfair or deceptive act or practice for funeral providers—that is, any business that sells or offers to sell both funeral goods and funeral services to the public—to (1) fail to furnish accurate itemized price information to funeral consumers; (2) misrepresent federal, state, local, or other requirements related to the provision of funeral goods and services; (3) require consumers to purchase items they do not want to buy; and (4) embalm deceased human remains for a fee without authorization.[13] Thus, among other things, compliance with the Funeral Rule requires that funeral providers furnish consumers with various price lists. For example, at the beginning of the discussion about arrangements for funeral goods and services, funeral providers must provide the consumer an itemized general price list. Funeral providers must also provide the consumer a casket price list before showing casket options. FTC staff opinions have also clarified various aspects of the Funeral Rule. For example, FTC staff opinions have provided that if a consumer purchases a casket from a third party vendor, a funeral provider cannot require a consumer's presence when the casket is delivered to the funeral home or charge a fee for certain services, such as storage of third-party caskets delivered a few days before they are needed.

Beginning in October 1994, the FTC initiated a test-shopping enforcement approach, called sweeps, targeting funeral homes in a particular region, state, or city. Under this approach, FTC staff in its regional offices, state investigators (such as those from offices of state attorneys general), or other volunteers (such as members of AARP—formerly known as the American Association of Retired Persons)[14] pose as consumers of funeral goods and services—thereby simulating a funeral transaction—to determine if the funeral home is in compliance with the Rule. In 1996, the

---

[12] GAO-03-757.

[13] See 16 C.F.R. §§ 453.2 (price disclosures); 453.3 (misrepresentations); 453.4 (required purchase of funeral goods or funeral services; and 453.5 (services provided without prior approval).

[14] AARP is a nonprofit, nonpartisan membership organization for people age 50 and over.

FTC implemented the Funeral Rule Offenders Program as a nonlitigation alternative to civil penalty actions for Rule violations.[15] Under this program, violators of the Funeral Rule are offered the option to attend the Funeral Rule Offenders Program. Those who choose to enroll in the program must agree to make voluntary payments to the U.S. Treasury equal to 0.8 percent of their average annual gross sales over the prior 3 years and participate in training designed to teach them how to comply with the Rule.

According to FTC staff, funeral homes are the segment of the death care industry most affected by the Funeral Rule, but federal legislation has been introduced that if enacted, could expand the scope of federal regulation. Since the Funeral Rule only applies to businesses providing both funeral goods and services, it tends to apply to funeral homes and not other segments of the death care industry that may provide either only merchandise or only services.[16] Under the proposed Bereaved Consumer's Bill of Rights Act of 2011, other segments of the death care industry, including cemeteries, would fall under federal regulation, and would further authorize both the FTC and state-level enforcement of the rules prescribed in accordance with the bill.[17] Specifically, the bill would require the FTC to prescribe rules that, among other things, (1) require cemeteries to disclose their written rules and regulations in a timely manner; (2) require clear and conspicuous disclosure of all fees and costs to be incurred in the future or at the time funeral goods or services are provided, and for any penalties that may be incurred for cancellation of prepaid contracts or transfer of them to other providers; and (3) require cemeteries to retain all extant records. The Bereaved Consumer's Bill of

---

[15] See 15 U.S.C. § 57b (authorizing FTC to commence a civil action against any person, partnership, or corporation for violating any rule proh biting unfair or deceptive acts or practices in a U.S. district court or any court of competent jurisdiction of a state).

[16] A 2009 FTC opinion (Opinion 09-1), explained that while the Funeral Rule generally does not apply to cemeteries, there may be some circumstances in which commercial cemeteries are funeral providers and are obliged to comply with the Rule. For example, if a commercial cemetery provides funeral services and offers or sells funeral goods, it would be obligated to comply with the Rule. A 2008 FTC opinion (Opinion 08-1) provided that a crematory must comply with the Funeral Rule if it offers and sells cremation services and any funeral goods, such as caskets, alternative containers, or urns. According to a 2004 FTC guide, the Funeral Rule also applies to pre-need and at-need funeral arrangements. Sellers of pre-need contracts that act on behalf of a funeral home, but do not provide funeral goods and service, must comply with the Rule.

[17] See H.R. 900, 112th Cong. (1st Sess. 2011).

Rights Act was referred to the House Committee on Energy and Commerce, Subcommittee on Commerce, Manufacturing and Trade, in March 2011, and no further action has been taken as of November 2011.

We also reported in 2003 that states vary in their approach to regulating the various segments of the death care industry, and that not all segments are subject to regulation in each state.[18] A 2009 FTC consumer guide provides an example of this, stating that laws of individual states govern the prepayment of funeral goods and services but that protections vary widely from state to state and some states offer little or no effective protection. In addition, some states have incorporated the Funeral Rule or aspects of the Funeral Rule into their statutes.

Consumer Costs and Industry Trends

While accurate national data are not readily available on how much consumers spend each year on death care transactions, in 2010, AARP reported that funeral expenses are one of the most expensive events in a person's life. The FTC reported in 2009 that a traditional funeral costs about $6,000, but that many funerals can cost well over $10,000. According to the National Center for Health Statistics, there were over 2.4 million deaths registered in the United States in 2007—the most recent year for which final data were available.[19] The Casket & Funeral Supply Association of America estimated that about 73 percent of the approximately 2.4 million deaths in 2007 resulted in a traditional casket burial. The National Funeral Directors Association reported that the average adult funeral cost was $6,560 in 2009.[20] Multiplying this figure by 1,752,000 (73 percent of the approximately 2.4 million deaths in 2009) provides an estimate of over $11.5 billion spent on funeral costs in the United States in 2009.

Although the Casket & Funeral Supply Association of America reported that the majority of people selected burial as the means of final disposition in 2007, trends in other methods of disposition are

---

[18] GAO-03-757.

[19] National Center for Health Statistics preliminary data show 2,473,018 deaths for 2008 and 2,436,682 deaths for 2009.

[20] This average excludes cemetery costs, including the cost of an outer burial container (such as a vault or a grave liner) that is required by many cemeteries, monument or marker costs, and miscellaneous cash-advance items, such as flowers and obituaries.

increasing—such as cremations or burials that that have minimal environmental impact. According to the Cremation Association of North America, the number and percentage of cremations is increasing, and the association projects that the national average could be over 55 percent by 2025. Several state and industry officials stated that the increase in cremations can partially be attributed to the downturn in the economy and increased social acceptance of cremation. With the rise in cremations, officials from the Cremation Association of North America stated that the weakened economy has contributed to crematories hiring cheap, untrained labor, which may create accidents or problems and that regulation of this segment of the industry has not kept pace with the increase in cremations. In addition, the use of environmentally friendly or "green" services or burials has received increasing media coverage, and some states have begun to discuss this issue and have proposed or passed legislation specifically addressing environmentally friendly or green burials. Examples of environmentally friendly burials can include the use of caskets or urns that are nontoxic and biodegradable and burials at "green" cemeteries in which the landscape is left in a natural state.

Finally, although media reports provide examples of incidents that have occurred in the industry, it is not possible to determine how prevalent these issues are across the death care industry. Our 1999 and 2003 reports on the death care industry found that comprehensive information on consumer complaints was not available because, among other reasons, (1) consumers can complain to a variety of entities and these entities may compile complaint data in various manners and (2) no single entity collects and compiles all complaint data.[21] Further, we reported that not all consumers who experience problems may file a complaint. For example, in our 1999 report, we stated that officials from organizations at all levels told us that factors, such as the emotional component of death, may inhibit a consumer from making a complaint. The challenges in using consumer complaints to determine the extent of the problems that may occur in the death care industry remain the same today.[22]

---

[21] GAO/GGD-99-156 and GAO-03-757.

[22] According to FTC staff, the agency has a Consumer Sentinel law enforcement database designed to be a central location for all consumer complaints, including complaints concerning the death care industry. The FTC staff said they are trying to get more agencies to use the database, but currently not everyone is using it.

Federal and State Regulation of the Death Care Industry and the Extent to Which It Has Changed Vary

Federal Regulatory Structure Largely Unchanged

The Funeral Rule has not changed since it went into effect in1994, and according to FTC staff, implementation of the Funeral Rule has generally remained the same since we last reported on the Rule in 2003. The FTC conducts undercover shopping through enforcement sweeps of funeral homes to ensure compliance with the Funeral Rule and to maintain consumer confidence.[23] Since the Funeral Rule Offenders Program was introduced in 1996, the FTC has shopped over 2,400 funeral homes of the approximately 20,000 funeral homes that FTC staff stated are in the United States.[24] The FTC reported an overall compliance rate of about 85 percent for all the sweeps conducted since 1996. Since 2004 through 2010, the yearly compliance rate fluctuated from 72 to 91 percent, as shown in table 1. FTC staff stated that they have no reliable basis to determine why the compliance rate is lower in recent years.

---

[23] The sweeps involve staff from the FTC's regional offices, who pose as consumers and visit funeral homes in a particular urban or rural geographic area to determine whether they are in compliance with the Funeral Rule.

[24] Some funeral homes have been shopped more than once.

Table 1: Number of Funeral Homes Shopped by the FTC, Number of Funeral Homes Found to Be Compliant or Noncompliant, and Associated Compliance Rates, 2004-2010

Year	Number of funeral homes sweeps were conducted at	Number of funeral homes in compliance	Number of funeral homes not in compliance	Compliance rate
2004	72	62	10	86%
2005	71	63	8	89%
2006	117	106	11	91%
2007	174	148	26	85%
2008	104	78	26	75%
2009	175	126	49	72%
2010	126	91	35	72%

Source: GAO analysis of Federal Trade Commission data.

When the Funeral Rule was first implemented, FTC staff stated that the typical violations they identified were related to not providing, or not providing in a timely manner, the general price list.[25] However, staff stated that this is much less of an issue today and that they now tend to uncover more issues with funeral homes not providing a casket price list before a consumer is shown caskets.[26] FTC staff stated that in 2007, they directed staff in their regional offices to conduct sweeps of funeral homes that had previously participated in the Funeral Rule Offenders Program. Of the 34 funeral homes that have since been revisited, FTC staff stated that most were in compliance with the Rule, but they are addressing compliance issues at a few of the funeral homes.[27] In 2011, the Department of Justice, at the request of the FTC, charged two funeral homes with violating the Funeral Rule. The FTC is seeking civil penalties against these funeral homes because they failed to provide consumers with price lists during an FTC sweep. According to FTC staff, these are the second and third cases (and the first since 1999) to be litigated since the Funeral Rule Offenders Program was implemented.

---

[25] The FTC does not maintain aggregate, national data on violations identified during sweeps. These data are maintained at the regional offices.

[26] In addition, FTC staff stated that they received complaints from third party sellers about funeral homes not accepting caskets. However, when FTC staff pursued the leads, they were unable to obtain sufficient evidence to support a law enforcement action.

[27] As of September 2011, information on these cases has not been released publicly because the cases are still open.

As we also reported in 1999,[28] FTC staff stated in September 2011 that they have coordinated with the states' attorney general's offices to conduct sweeps of funeral homes for Funeral Rule compliance and that this coordination has been positive. However, the FTC also noted that in some states, the attorney general's offices do not have the resources to assist with the sweeps. Of the three states' attorney general's offices we contacted that had helped the FTC conduct sweeps in their respective states, all generally reported that the coordination efforts were positive. Further, officials from two offices stated that their involvement in the sweeps required minimal resources from their offices, but an official from another office stated that their office's coordination resulted in about 75 hours worth of staff time and about $2,000 in travel expenses. According to one attorney general's office, the last funeral sweep it conducted with the FTC occurred around the year 2000, and officials stated that it was beneficial in that it identified violations, highlighted the importance of complying with the Funeral Rule for providers, and helped to educate consumers. According to an official from another state's attorney general's office, their office coordinated with the FTC on sweeps of funeral homes twice—once in 1995 and once in 2010—and noted that these efforts were valuable because they helped identify issues that may not have been brought to their attention otherwise. However, an official from this office also noted that funeral home sweeps could be done more systematically—possibly selecting funeral homes based on a sampling method—and more frequently.

In our 1999 report, we recommended that the FTC review possible approaches to determine the most cost-effective means for the FTC to conduct sweeps that would result in both a more convincing sample of funeral providers and implement a plan for carrying out such an approach in a systematic manner.[29] In August 2003, FTC staff told us that that they constantly evaluate the methods by which the Funeral Rule may be enforced and reported that they make decisions about their approach yearly as part of their strategic plan. In September 2011, FTC staff stated that they continue to discuss Funeral Rule sweeps as part of their strategic planning, and as such, hold conference calls with each region to discuss where they will conduct sweeps. Furthermore, FTC staff stated that their goal is to conduct sweeps at a variety of funeral homes in

---

[28] GAO/GGD-99-156.

[29] GAO/GGD-99-156.

various locations. However, according to these staff, the number of sweeps they conduct is also driven by resources, including the availability of staff to conduct the sweeps and funds so that staff can travel to various locations. They explained that funeral home sweeps can be resource intensive because staff who pose as shoppers have to travel to the area of the sweep to physically visit funeral homes, gather the information and record it shortly after the visit is conducted, reshop the funeral home if violations are uncovered, and then take any necessary actions to secure compliance.

State Regulation of the Industry Varies by State and Industry Segment

States vary in their approach to regulating the death care industry across states and across industry segments. Overall, most of the state regulators we surveyed reported having rules or regulations specific to funeral homes, cemeteries, crematories, and pre-need sellers; however, more than two-thirds of the state regulators who responded to our 2011 survey reported that they did not have rules or regulations specific to third party sellers of funeral goods, as shown in figure 1.

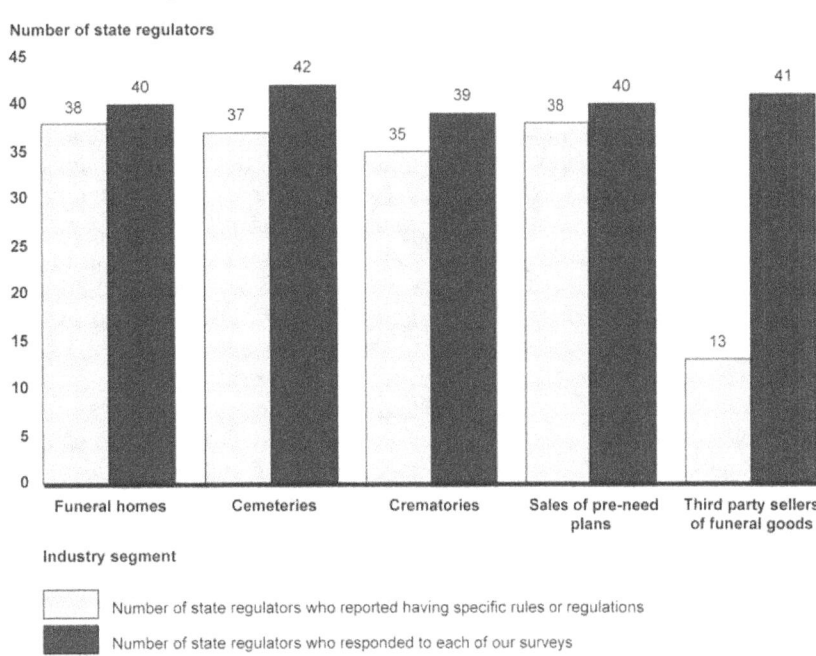

Figure 1: Number of State Regulators Who Responded to Our 2011 Surveys and Number Who Reported That Their State Has Specific Rules or Regulations

Number of state regulators

Industry segment

☐ Number of state regulators who reported having specific rules or regulations

■ Number of state regulators who responded to each of our surveys

Source: GAO surveys of state regulators.

Further, as highlighted by state regulators from our case study states, what it means to regulate can vary from state to state. For example, in Colorado, funeral homes are required to register with the state but funeral directors and embalmers are not, while in Tennessee, funeral homes, funeral directors, and embalmers are all required to be licensed, and funeral homes are to be inspected once a year. The following sections provide more specific information on the regulation of each segment of the death care industry—(1) funeral homes, (2) cemeteries, (3) crematories, (4) pre-need funeral plans, and (5) third party sellers of funeral goods. Much of the information below was obtained through our surveys of state regulators, and although we obtained about an 81 percent average response rate on our five surveys, not every state regulator provided a response to each question. As a result, the total number of respondents for each question may vary.

See appendixes III through VII for more detailed information on the five case study states' regulation of each of the industry segments.[30] To view the surveys and the responding state regulators' answers to the survey questions, go to GAO-12-91SP.

Funeral Homes, Funeral Directors, and Embalmers

As stated above, the majority of state regulators reported having specific rules or regulations that address all funeral homes that operate in their states. Specifically, of the 40 state regulators who responded to our 2011 survey on the regulation of funeral homes, 38 reported having specific rules or regulations.[31] Arizona was the only state that reported that some funeral homes were exempt from regulation, specifically, funeral homes on tribal grounds. State regulators who provided data on the number of funeral homes in their states reported having between 18 and 1,874 funeral homes operating in their states in 2011.

In addition, the majority of state regulators also reported that funeral homes, funeral directors, and embalmers are required to be licensed in their respective states.[32] For example, of the state regulators who responded to these issues on our survey, 37 of the 38 reported that funeral homes are required to be licensed. State regulators reported that licenses were required to be renewed at various frequencies, if at all, although most reported that licenses had to be renewed every at least once every 1 or 2 years. In four of our five case study states, funeral directors and embalmers are required to obtain a license to operate and such applicants are generally required to (1) pay a fee, (2) pass an exam, (3) obtain some level of education, and (4) have some experience—which may be as an intern or an apprentice. Licensees in each of these four states are required to renew their licenses once every 2 years.

---

[30] For each of these appendixes, we group information for each of the industry segments into several categories, such as licensing requirements and inspection and audit requirements. Each state may use different terminology and we explain this in the appendix text, but for consistency, the categories are generally the same across each of these appendixes.

[31] One of the state regulators who reported not having specific rules or regulations addressing funeral homes did, however, report that the state has specific rules and regulations addressing funeral directors and embalmers.

[32] In some states, such as Illinois, Indiana, and Pennsylvania, state regulators reported that one license covers both funeral directors and embalmers.

With respect to inspections, 35 of the 38 state regulators who responded to this issue on our survey reported that the inspection of funeral homes was required, although the frequency of these required inspections varied. In our case study states, for example, Oregon requires that funeral homes be inspected every 2 years and Tennessee requires funeral homes to be inspected once a year.[33] In Colorado and Illinois, state regulators stated that funeral homes are not inspected on a regular basis, although regulators have the authority to do so. Further, the 32 state regulators who responded to our question regarding the number of inspectors they have reported having between one and nine inspectors. However, only 1 of the 26 state regulators who provided information on the percentage of time their inspectors spend inspecting funeral homes reported that the state's inspectors spend 100 percent of their time inspecting funeral homes.[34]

As a result of inspections or other enforcement mechanisms, state regulators reported identifying a wide variety of violations and taking various types of enforcement actions against funeral homes, funeral directors, and embalmers. Of the 38 state regulators who responded to this issue on our survey, 33 reported tracking violations of funeral homes, funeral directors, and embalmers. Twenty-two state regulators provided data on the approximate number of violations identified since 2008, with 14 reporting that there were fewer than 40 violations in their respective states.[35] Of the 26 state regulators who provided narrative responses to our survey about the most frequent violations they identified, the most frequent were violations related to licensing, such as unlicensed or unregistered practice, with 10 state regulators reporting this as being a common violation. Other violations reported by state regulators included

---

[33] In Tennessee, for example, inspectors use a standard report form in conducting inspections and inspect for cleanliness, proper documentation of licensing records, and Funeral Rule compliance, among other things. In addition, inspectors will compare the funeral homes' price lists to invoices for a select number of sales to ensure that funeral homes are charging according to their price lists.

[34] State regulators who responded to this issue generally reported that inspectors also spend some of their time inspecting other facilities or conducting other work. Other facilities that inspectors were reported to inspect include crematories, cemeteries, and food establishments. Other work that state regulators reported that inspectors conducted included licensing and administrative work.

[35] Of the remaining state regulators who provided responses, 4 reported that there were between 100 and 200 violations, 3 reported between 300 and 500 violations, and 1 reported over 1,800 violations since 2008.

those related to unprofessional conduct, FTC Funeral Rule violations, reporting deficiencies, and service issues.[36] Finally, 34 of 38 state regulators who responded to our question about taking enforcement actions against funeral homes, funeral directors, or embalmers reported that they have taken some actions since 2008, including actions ranging from notices of non-compliance and letters of reprimand to suspension of licenses and civil or criminal prosecutions.

States also varied in the number of consumer complaints they received regarding funeral homes, funeral directors, and embalmers. Of the 39 state regulators who responded to this issue on our survey, 33 reported that their state tracks data on consumer complaints. For the years 2008, 2009, and 2010, state regulators reported that their state received between 0 and 300 complaints, approximately, each year—although the vast majority reported that their state received fewer than 100 complaints each year.[37] Common complaints reported in our case study states included unlicensed practice, overcharging, and customer service concerns. Further, conducting investigations of legitimate consumer complaints was most frequently reported by state regulators who responded to our survey as being the consumer protection that was most effective in protecting consumers.

Cemeteries and Cemetery Operators

Most state regulators reported having specific rules or regulations that address some cemeteries that operate in their states. Specifically, of the 42 state regulators who responded to our 2011 survey on the regulation of cemeteries, 37 reported having rules or regulations specific to cemeteries. Further, of the 36 state regulators who responded to the question regarding whether all cemeteries are subject to state regulation, 29 reported that some cemeteries were exempt from regulation in their state. Examples of cemeteries that were exempt from regulation in some states include religious, municipal, family, private, and public cemeteries.

---

[36] States do not necessarily categorize violations in the same manner, and not all states track violations in the same manner.

[37] Specifically, of the state regulators who provided data on the number of complaints the state received each year, 20 of 24 reported fewer than 100 complaints in 2008, 19 of 25 reported fewer than 100 complaints in 2009, and 21 of 26 reported fewer than 100 complaints in 2010. Not all the state regulators who reported tracking data on consumer complaints provided the total number of complaints for each year. In addition, consumers may have submitted complaints to an agency other than the state regulatory agency that responded to our survey.

The number of cemeteries operating in the states is not always known, as 18 of the 37 state regulators who responded to this issue reported that they did not maintain data on the number of cemeteries that operate in their states. Five state regulators provided data on the number of cemeteries that operated in their states—reporting having as few as 124 to as many as 3,600 cemeteries operating in their states.

In addition, many state regulators reported that some cemeteries and cemetery operators are required to be licensed in their respective states. Specifically, of the state regulators who responded to these issues on our survey,

- 22 of the 37 reported that some but not all cemeteries are required to be licensed, 10 reported that no license is required, 4 reported that all cemeteries are required to be licensed, and 1 checked "No response"[38] and
- 20 of the 37 reported that cemetery operators are not required to be licensed, 11 reported that some but not all cemetery operators are required to be licensed, 1 reported that all are required to be licensed, and 5 checked "No response."[39]

State regulators reported that licenses were required to be renewed at various frequencies, if at all. In our case study states, for example, Tennessee requires cemeteries to renew their license once a year, while Oregon requires cemeteries to renew their licenses once every 2 years.

With respect to inspection, 21 of the 37 state regulators who responded to this issue on our survey reported that inspections of cemeteries were not required, and those that did require them reported that the frequency of the required inspections varied. In our case study states, for example, Oregon requires cemeteries to be inspected once every 2 years, while in Wisconsin state regulators have the authority to conduct inspections, but according to Wisconsin regulators, these are not done on a regular basis.

---

[38] For example, some state regulators who responded that some but not all cemeteries were required to be licensed noted that some cemeteries, such as religious, public, family, and municipal cemeteries, were exempt from their state's licensing requirements.

[39] In those states in which cemetery operators were not required to be licensed, state regulators provided additional clarification on their state's requirements. For example, two state regulators reported that although cemetery operators did not need to be licensed, they were required to be registered.

The 12 state regulators who responded to our survey question regarding the number of inspectors available to inspect cemeteries reported having between zero and nine inspectors. However, 1 of the 11 state regulators who provided information on what percentage of their time their inspectors spend inspecting cemeteries reported that their inspectors spend 100 percent of their time inspecting cemeteries.[40]

As a result of inspections or other enforcement mechanisms, state regulators reported identifying a variety of violations and taking various types of enforcement actions against cemeteries and cemetery operators. Of the 34 state regulators who responded to this issue on our survey, 18 reported tracking violations of cemeteries and cemetery operators, and 11 reported on the approximate number of violations identified since 2008—which ranged from 0 to 122 in their respective states.[41] Of the 16 state regulators who provided narrative responses to our survey about the most frequent violations they identify, violations included those related to (1) record keeping, (2) maintenance, (3) unprofessional conduct, and (4) licensing.[42] Finally, 22 of 36 state regulators who responded to our question about taking enforcement actions against cemeteries or cemetery operators reported that they have taken some actions since 2008, including actions ranging from notices of non-compliance to monetary fines and civil or criminal prosecutions. However, as pointed out by one of our case study state regulators, although they receive complaints about cemetery maintenance issues, these issues don't normally develop into an actual case that could result in an enforcement action.

States also reported receiving some consumer complaints regarding cemeteries and cemetery operators. Of the 41 state regulators who

---

[40] State regulators who responded to this issue generally reported that inspectors also spend some of their time inspecting other facilities or conducting other work. Other facilities that inspectors were reported to inspect include funeral homes, crematories, and companies that sell pre-need plans. Other work that state regulators reported that inspectors conducted included licensing and administrative work.

[41] Specifically, 3 state regulators reported that there were no violations, 4 reported between 1 and 15 violations, 3 reported between 50 and 100 violations, and 1 reported 122 violations since 2008. Not all the state regulators who reported tracking data on violations provided the total number of violations since 2008.

[42] States do not necessarily categorize violations in the same manner and not all states track violations in the same manner.

responded to this issue on our survey, 25 state regulators reported that their state tracks data on consumer complaints. For the years 2008, 2009, and 2010, state regulators reported that their state received between 0 and 113 complaints, approximately, in each respective year regarding cemeteries or cemetery operators, with the majority reporting that their state received 40 complaints or fewer each year.[43] Common complaints reported in our case study states included maintenance issues and incorrect monument placements. Conducting investigations of legitimate consumer complaints was most frequently reported by state regulators as being the consumer protection that was most effective in protecting consumers.

Crematories and Crematory Operators

Most state regulators reported having rules or regulations that specifically address crematories that operate in their states. Specifically, of the 39 state regulators who responded to our 2011 survey on the regulation of crematories, 35 reported having specific rules or regulations. Four of those that reported having rules or regulations also reported that some crematories were exempt from regulation. The types of crematories that were reported to be exempt included pet crematories and a university medical center crematory. State regulators who provided data on the number of crematories reported having between 7 and 208 crematories operating in their states in 2011.

In addition, most state regulators reported that crematories are required to be licensed in their respective states but varied on whether a license was required for crematory operators. Of the 35 state regulators who responded to this issue on the survey,

- 28 reported that all crematories are required to be licensed, 4 reported that some but not all are required to be licensed, and 3 reported that no license is required[44] and

---

[43] Specifically, of the state regulators who provided data on the number of complaints the state received each year, 13 of 17 reported fewer than 40 complaints in 2008, 14 of 19 reported fewer than 40 complaints in 2009 and 2010. Not all the state regulators who reported tracking data on consumer complaints provided the total number of complaints for each year. In addition, consumers may have submitted complaints to an agency other than the state regulatory agency that responded to our survey.

[44] For example, some state regulators who responded that some but not all crematories were required to be licensed noted that some crematories, such as pet crematories, were exempt from their state's licensing requirements.

- 16 reported that all crematory operators are required to be licensed, 4 reported that some but not all are required to be licensed, and 15 reported that no license was required.[45]

State regulators reported that licenses were required to be renewed at various frequencies, if at all, although the majority reported that licenses had to be renewed at least once every 1 or 2 years. In our case study states, for example, Wisconsin requires crematory operators to renew their registration once every 2 years, while Illinois has no requirement for crematory operators to renew their licenses.

With respect to inspections, most state regulators reported that inspections of crematories were required. Specifically, 28 of the 34 state regulators who responded to this issue in our survey reported that the inspection of crematories is required, and although the frequency of the required inspections varied, about half required crematories to be inspected at least once a year. Of our case study states, for example, Tennessee requires crematories to be inspected once a year, Oregon requires them to be inspected every 2 years, and according to state regulators in Wisconsin, inspections are done if there is a complaint. The 27 state regulators who responded to our question regarding the number of inspectors they have to inspect crematories reported having between one and nine inspectors. However, 20 of the 22 state regulators who provided information on what percentage of time their inspectors spend inspecting crematories reported that their inspectors spend less than 25 percent of their time inspecting crematories.[46]

As a result of inspections or other enforcement mechanisms, states reported identifying a variety of violations and taking various types of enforcement actions against crematories and crematory operators. Of the

---

[45] In those states in which crematory operators were not required to be licensed, state regulators provided additional clarification on their state's requirements. For example, several stated that the crematory operator did not need to be licensed but that a licensed funeral director was required to be in charge of the crematory. State regulators from another state reported that although crematory operators did not need to be licensed, they were required to be registered.

[46] State regulators who responded to this issue generally reported that inspectors also spend some of their time inspecting other facilities or conducting other work. Other facilities that inspectors were reported to inspect include funeral homes and cemeteries. Other work that state regulators reported that inspectors conducted included investigating consumer complaints and administrative work.

35 state regulators who responded to this issue on our survey, 31 reported tracking violations of crematories and crematory operators. Twenty-three state regulators provided data on the approximate number of violations identified since 2008—10 reported no violations, 9 reported 1 to 3 violations, and the remaining 4 reported 15 to 43 violations.[47] Of the 16 state regulators who provided narrative responses to our survey about the most frequent violations they identify, violations included those related to (1) record keeping, (2) the handling of bodies or human remains, (3) obtaining the proper authorization to cremate or issues with following the wishes of the person with control over final disposition, and (4) licensing, such as unlicensed or unregistered practice. Finally, 12 of 34 state regulators who responded to our question about taking enforcement actions against crematories or crematory operators reported that they have taken some actions since 2008, including actions ranging from notices of non-compliance to monetary fines and civil or criminal prosecutions.

Most states also track consumer complaints and reported receiving fewer than 10 consumer complaints a year. Specifically, 32 of the 39 state regulators who responded to this issue on our survey reported that their state tracked consumer complaints. For the years 2008, 2009, and 2010, state regulators reported that their state received between 0 and 7 complaints, approximately, in each respective year regarding crematories or crematory operators, with 0 being the most frequent response for each year.[48] Specifically, in 2008 and 2009, more than 60 percent of the state regulators reported that their state received no complaints and in 2010 more than 45 percent reported that their state received no complaints. Complaints reported in our case study states included procedural concerns, such as cremating without proper identification tags and not obtaining proper authorization before cremation, and environmental concerns. Conducting investigations of legitimate consumer complaints was most frequently reported by state regulators as being the consumer protection that was most effective in protecting consumers.

---

[47] Not all the state regulators who reported tracking data on violations provided the total number of violations since 2008.

[48] Not all the state regulators who reported tracking data on consumer complaints provided the total number of complaints for each year. In addition, consumers may have submitted complaints to an agency other than the state regulatory agency that responded to our survey.

Sales of Pre-Need Plans

Most state regulators reported having rules or regulations that specifically address sales of pre-need plans—plans that involve the prearrangement and prepurchase of funeral and cemetery goods and services.[49] Specifically, of the 40 state regulators who responded to our survey on the regulation of the sales of pre-need plans, 38 reported having specific rules or regulations. Seven of the 37 state regulators who responded to the question regarding whether all pre-need sales are subject to state regulation reported that some pre-need sales were exempt from regulation in their state.[50] State regulators reported that the types of pre-need sales that are exempt from regulation in their state included third party sales and sales of cemetery plots. State regulators who provided data on the number of sellers of pre-need plans—which can include companies and their sales agents—in their state reported having up to 1,167 companies that sold pre-need plans and up to 1,697 individual sales agents operating in their states in 2011.

Most state regulators reported that sellers of pre-need plans—which includes companies and their sales agents—are required to be licensed in their respective states. Specifically, of the 38 state regulators who responded to this issue on our survey, 27 reported that all sellers of pre-need plans are required to be licensed, 8 reported that some but not all had to be licensed, and 2 reported that no license was required.[51] State regulators reported that licenses were required to be renewed at various frequencies, if at all, although the majority reported that licenses had to be renewed at least once a year. In our case study states, for example, Colorado requires pre-need sellers to renew their licenses every year, Tennessee and Wisconsin require them to renew every 2 years, and

---

[49] For our survey, we noted that the term "pre-need funeral plans" refers to the purchase of funeral goods and services to be provided at a later date when death occurs. It does not refer to the purchase of a final expense insurance policy from which the beneficiary would claim and receive payment on the policy and be responsible for paying any costs for funeral goods and services on behalf of the deceased. Although funds from pre-need contracts tend to be placed in insurance policies or trust funds, state regulators from our case study states generally reported that they have seen more insurance-funded pre-need contracts compared to trust-funded ones. For more information on pre-need plans, see app. II.

[50] Specifically, 34 state regulators reported that their state's rules and regulations cover sales of pre-need plans made at funeral homes, 27 reported that their state's rules and regulations cover sales of pre-need plans made at cemeteries, and 18 reported that their state's rules and regulations cover sales of pre-need plans made by third party sellers.

[51] One state regulator who responded to this question checked "No response."

there is no requirement in Illinois for pre-need sellers to renew their licenses. In addition, 17 state regulators reported that sellers of pre-need plans are required to be associated with a funeral home or cemetery and 8 reported that a seller must be a licensed funeral director.

In our case study states, various methods were used to measure pre-need sellers' compliance with state laws and regulations. For example, Colorado, Illinois, Oregon, Tennessee, and Wisconsin require pre-need sellers to submit annual reports that state regulators review for various things, such as if funds were properly trusted and abnormal fluctuation in funds. Tennessee also examines pre-need sellers every year, and Colorado also examines the records of pre-need sellers every 5 years. Twenty-five of the 38 state regulators who responded to our question about violations reported tracking violations regarding the sales of pre-need plans. Fifteen state regulators provided data on the approximate number of violations identified since 2008—5 reported no violations, 4 reported between 1 to 5 violations, 4 reported between 50 and 134 violations, 1 reported 379 violations, and another reported 1,578 violations during this time.[52] Of the 17 state regulators who provided narrative responses to our survey about the most frequent violations they identify, violations related to improper trusting or misappropriating funds were frequently cited by state regulators as being a common violation. Other violations mentioned included record keeping issues, unlicensed practice, and contract issues.[53] Finally, 24 of 38 state regulators who responded to our question about taking enforcement actions against sellers of pre-need plans reported that they have taken some actions since 2008, including actions ranging from notices of non-compliance to revocation or suspension of licenses and civil or criminal prosecutions. According to a state regulator in one of our case study states, although the state has revoked about four to five licenses in the last 10 years with the assistance of the attorney general's office, the state regulatory agency is very limited in the disciplinary actions it is authorized to take and the process is very slow and costly.

---

[52] Not all the state regulators who reported tracking data on violations provided the total number of violations since 2008.

[53] States do not necessarily categorize violations in the same manner and not all states track violations in the same manner.

In addition, some state regulators reported having other consumer protections in their states with respect to sales of pre-need plans—including consumer protection accounts, trusting requirements, and cancellation and transferability of contracts—although these also varied by state. The following briefly discusses each.

Consumer protection account. A consumer protection account collects and maintains funds for the benefit and protection of consumers of pre-need plans. Of the 40 state regulators who responded to this issue on our survey, 10 reported that their state has a consumer protection fund that would protect consumers of pre-need plans who suffered financial losses because of issues such as fraud, default, or insolvency. Three of our five case study states reported maintaining consumer protection accounts, although the purpose of these accounts varied. For example, in Illinois and Oregon, funds from these accounts are used for consumer restitution, while in Tennessee, funds from this account are used to support general operation and expenses of the state regulator, as well as any receivership actions initiated. The 9 state regulators who provided data on the maximum amount of funds available in their state's consumer protection account since 2003 reported having between $30,000 and $1.5 million.

Trusting requirements. Trusting requirements refer to the amounts of funds from pre-need sales that are required to be deposited into a trust account. Whereas each state's laws or regulations will dictate applicable trusting requirements, in general, the seller of pre-need goods or services must deposit a specified percentage of a pre-need sale into a trust account to cover the costs of funeral goods and services at the time of death. Of the state regulators who responded to this issue on our survey, 33 of 38 reported that they have specific trusting requirements, although the percentage of pre-need sales revenue that is required to be trusted for funeral and cemetery goods and services varies. Specifically, as shown in table 2, trusting requirements for funeral goods and services tend to be higher than those for cemetery goods and services across all states whose regulators responded to this issue on our survey.

Table 2: Trusting Requirements: Required Percentage of Total Value of Purchased Pre-Need Goods and Services That Must be Placed in Trust for Five Types of Goods and Services, by Number of States in Each Category, as Reported in 2011

Percentage of funds that are required to be trusted	Funeral goods	Funeral services	Cemetery goods	Cemetery services	Third party sellers
Zero percent	—	—	2	2	4
One to 19 percent	—	—	1	2	—
Twenty to 39 percent	1	—	2	1	—
Forty to 59 percent	2	—	5	3	1
Sixty to 79 percent	3	3	4	4	1
Eighty to 99 percent	9	10	3	5	5
One hundred percent or more	15	17	6	8	8

Source: GAO survey of state regulators of the sales of pre-need plans.

Once funds are deposited, trustees in some states may withdraw funds from the trust for things such as administrative fees. Specifically, of the state regulators who responded to this issue on our survey,

- 14 reported that administrative fees can be withdrawn,
- 9 reported that no funds may ever be withdrawn,
- 7 reported that a specified percentage of the interest can be withdrawn,
- 5 reported that a specified percentage or amount of trust funds dollars may be withdrawn,
- 3 reported that there are no specific requirements, and
- 2 reported that any funds over 100 percent of the purchase price can be withdrawn.

Canceling and transferring pre-need contracts. Of the 39 state regulators who responded to the question on our survey about cancellation requirements, regulators frequently reported that if a consumer cancels a pre-need contract, the consumer is entitled to receive the principal and interest, as shown in table 3.

Table 3: Number of State Regulators Who Reported Different Refund Requirements for Cancellations of Pre-Need Contracts, as Reported in 2011

If purchasers of pre-need funeral plans within your state cancel their pre-need contracts, what refunds, if any, are they entitled to from their investment?	Number of state regulators
They are entitled to receive the principal they invested, plus any interest that has accrued	12
This depends on the individual contract	5
Other[a]	7
They are entitled to receive the principal they invested, less any administrative and/or revocation fees	4
They are entitled to receive the principal they invested, plus any interest that has accrued, and less any administrative and/or revocation fees	4
They are not entitled to receive any refund	2
They are entitled to receive only the principal they invested	2
No response	3

Source: GAO survey of state regulators of the sales of pre-need plans.

[a]State regulators who responded "other" provided various explanations of their cancellation requirements. For example, in Florida, how much is refunded depends upon when the contract is cancelled, and in Texas, the amount refunded depends on whether the contract is trust funded or insurance funded.

With respect to consumers' right to transfer pre-need contracts to another state, of the 40 state regulators responding to this issue on our survey, 12 reported that there are no specific requirements in their state, 11 reported that consumers are permitted to transfer their contract to another state and no penalties will apply, 8 reported that consumers can transfer the contract but penalties may apply, 4 reported that consumers are not permitted to transfer their contracts to another state, and 5 checked "No response."

The amount of funds invested in pre-need plans is not always known because not all states track the amount of funds invested in these plans. Eighteen of the 39 state regulators who reported on whether their state tracked the amount of funds invested in pre-need plans stated that they did track this amount, and 9 reported the amount of funds invested in pre-need plans in 2010, which ranged from $100,000 to $2.9 billion. (See app. II for more information on this issue.) Based on information obtained from our case study states, individual contracts may also be tracked in states. In Oregon, for example, sellers of pre-need plans are required to provide numbers for each contract in consecutive order to help ensure that each contract can be tracked.

Finally, most state regulators reported that they track consumer complaints regarding sales of pre-need plans and reported receiving some complaints. Specifically, 27 of the 39 state regulators who responded to this issue on our survey reported that their state tracks consumer complaints. For the years 2008, 2009, and 2010, state regulators generally reported that their state received between 0 and 25 complaints, approximately, in each respective year regarding sellers of pre-need plans—although 2 state regulators reported that their state received more than 25 complaints in all 3 years, with 180 complaints being the highest number reported in all 3 years.[54] Common complaints reported in case study states included failure to trust funds and contract disputes. Conducting investigations of legitimate consumer complaints was most frequently reported by state regulators who responded to this issue as being the consumer protection that was most effective in protecting consumers.

Third Party Sellers of Funeral Goods

Most state regulators reported that they did not have rules or regulations specifically addressing third party sellers of funeral goods—which includes retailers of caskets, urns, and monuments that are not affiliated with a funeral home or cemetery. Specifically, of the 41 state regulators who responded to our survey on the regulation of third party sellers, 13 reported having specific rules or regulations, although 1 of these 13 reported that the specific rule or regulation was that all third party sales were prohibited or were restricted.[55] Further, of the 12 state regulators who responded to this issue on our survey, 5 reported that some third party sellers were exempt from regulation in their state. State regulators reported that various third party sales were exempt, including cemetery merchandise sales and immediate-need sales of funeral goods.

---

[54] Specifically, of the state regulators who provided data on the number of complaints the state received each year, 12 of 14 reported 25 or fewer complaints in 2008, and 13 of 15 reported 25 or fewer complaints in 2009 and 2010. Not all the state regulators who reported tracking data on consumer complaints provided the total number of complaints for each year. In addition, consumers may have submitted complaints to an agency other than the state regulatory agency that responded to our survey.

[55] Three state regulators who responded to this question checked "No response." Although potentially in conflict with the Funeral Rule, one state regulator we surveyed reported that their state prohibits or restricts third party sales. A state regulator from one of our case study states told us that their state law may be in conflict with the Funeral Rule because funeral homes did not have to accept third party caskets. GAO did not undertake to determine whether the practice of any state conflicts with the Funeral Rule as part of this review.

Of the states that have specific rules or regulations for third party sellers, states varied on their licensing requirements. Specifically, of the 12 state regulators who responded to our survey question about licensing requirements, 4 reported that all third party sellers are required to be licensed, 3 reported that some were required to be licensed, and 5 reported that no license was required. According to the seven state regulators who reported that licenses were required, they varied in how often licenses had to be renewed.

State regulators reported identifying some violations.[56] Of the 5 state regulators who provided narrative responses to our survey about the most frequent violations they identify, violations related to not properly trusting funds and failure to provide services were among the violations reported.[57] State regulators also reported receiving some consumer complaints. Of the 41 state regulators who responded to our survey question about consumer complaints, 10 reported that their state tracks consumer complaints.[58] State regulators reported that their state received between 0 and 4 complaints, approximately, regarding third party sellers in 2008 and 2010, and between 0 and 10 complaints in 2009.[59]

In Both 2003 and 2011 States Reported Varied Regulatory Requirements, with Specific Rules or Regulations Most Consistently Reported for Funeral Homes

The extent to which state regulators reported that their state (1) had specific rules or regulations, (2) required licensing, and (3) required inspections in both 2003 and 2011 varied by industry segment.[60] For

[56] Six state regulators reported that their state tracks violations. Two state regulators provided data on the total number of violations there had been in their state—both reporting that there were none since 2008.

[57] States do not necessarily categorize violations in the same manner and not all states track violations in the same manner.

[58] Twenty-four state regulators reported that their state did not maintain data on consumer complaints, and 7 checked "No response."

[59] Not all the state regulators who reported tracking data on consumer complaints provided the total number of complaints for each year. In addition, consumers may have submitted complaints to an agency other than the state regulatory agency that responded to our survey.

[60] Although states may not have changed their requirements on whether a license or inspection is required, they may have made changes to how this requirement is implemented or enforced. Also, differences from year to year could be attributable to the fact that different states responded in 2003 and 2011. Specifically, depending on the industry segment, 85 to 98 percent of those that responded to our 2011 survey also responded to our survey in 2003.

example, with regard to funeral homes, 45 of 48 state regulators (94 percent) who responded to our 2003 survey reported that their state had specific rules or regulations for funeral homes, while 38 of 40 state regulators (95 percent) reported this in 2011. In contrast, with regard to cemeteries, 34 of 44 state regulators (77 percent) who responded to our 2003 survey reported that their state had specific rules or regulations for cemeteries, whereas 37 of 42 state regulators (88 percent) reported this in 2011. Figure 2 shows the number of state regulators who responded to our surveys and the number who reported that their state had specific rules or regulations for each of the industry segments in 2003 and 2011.

Figure 2: Extent to Which State Regulators Reported That Their State Had Rules or Regulations Specific to Each Industry Segment, 2003 and 2011

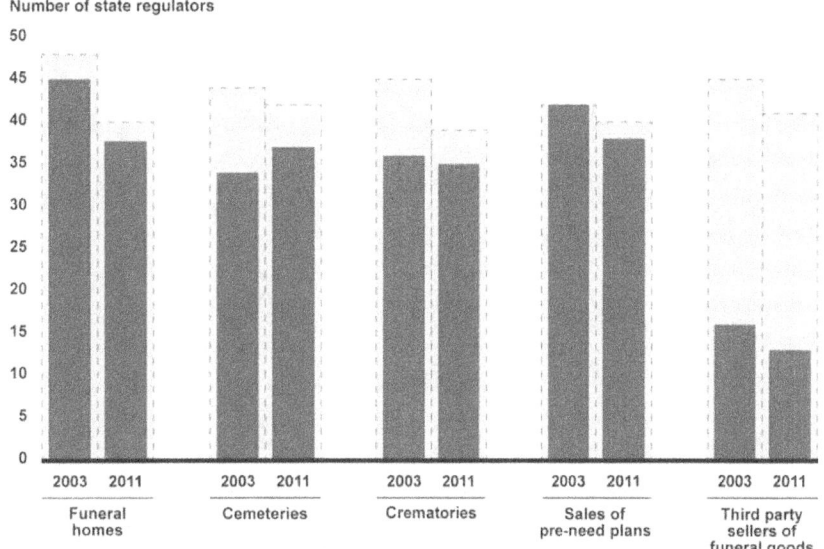

Number of state regulators

Industry segment

Number of state regulators who reported having specific rules or regulations

Number of state regulators who responded to each of our surveys

Source: GAO survey of state regulators.

Note: Differences from year to year could be attributable to the fact that different states responded in 2003 and 2011. Specifically, depending on the industry segment, 85 to 98 percent of those that responded to our 2011 survey also responded to our survey in 2003.

The extent to which state regulators reported that their state required licenses also varied by industry segment between 2003 and 2011. For example, in 2003 and 2011, almost all of the state regulators who responded to our surveys reported that their state required all funeral homes to be licensed. Specifically, 42 of 43 state regulators (98 percent) who responded to our 2003 survey reported that their state required all funeral homes to be licensed, while 37 of 38 state regulators (97 percent) reported this in 2011. In contrast, there was more variation in state's licensing requirement for cemetery operators in 2003 compared to 2011. For example, whereas 17 of 33 state regulators (52 percent) who responded to our 2003 survey reported that their state did not require cemetery operators to be licensed, 20 of 32 state regulators (63 percent) reported this in 2011. Figure 3 shows the number of state regulators who reported their state's licensing requirements by each of the industry segments in 2003 and 2011.

Figure 3: Extent to Which State Regulators Reported That Their State Had Licensing Requirements by Industry Segment, 2003 and 2011

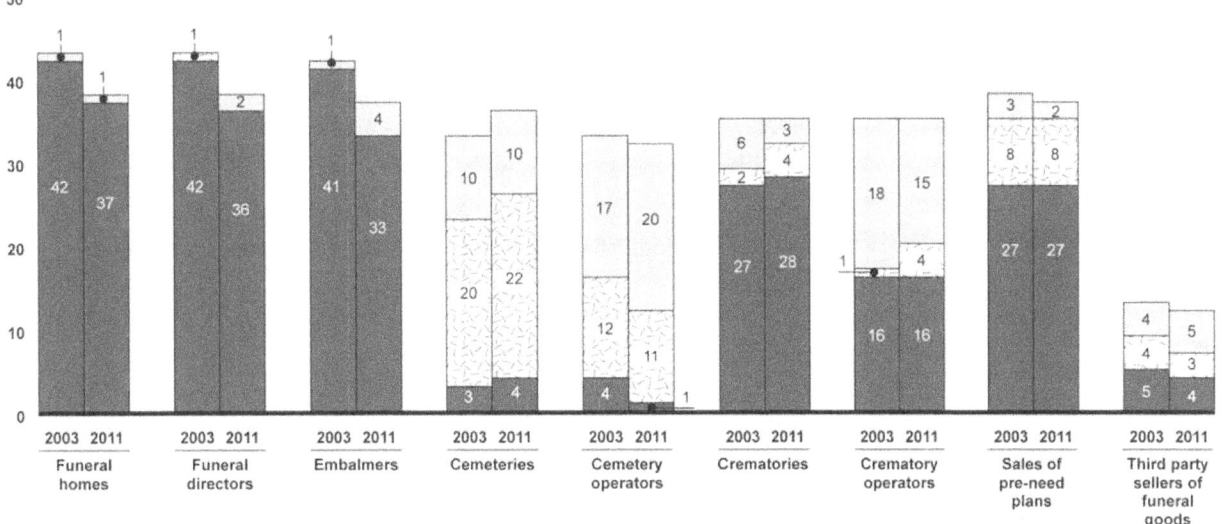

Number of state regulators

No license is required

Some but not all must be licensed

All must be licensed

Source: GAO survey of state regulators.

Note: Differences from year to year could be attributable to the fact that different states responded in 2003 and 2011. Specifically, depending on the industry segment, 85 to 98 percent of those hat responded to our 2011 survey also responded to our survey in 2003.

Furthermore, the number of state regulators who reported that their state required inspections varied by industry segment between 2003 and 2011. Specifically, 19 of 33 state regulators (58 percent) who responded to our 2003 survey reported that their state did not require the inspection of cemeteries, while 21 of 37 state regulators (57 percent) reported this in 2011. By comparison, with respect to the inspection of funeral homes and crematories,

- 37 of 43 state regulators (86 percent) who responded to our 2003 survey reported that their state required the inspection of funeral homes, while 35 of the 38 state regulators (92 percent) reported this in 2011, and

- 33 of 36 state regulators (92 percent) who responded to our 2003 survey reported that their state required the inspection of crematories, while 28 of the 34 state regulators (82 percent) reported this in 2011.

Many state regulators who responded to our 2011 survey also reported that their states made changes to their laws or regulations since 2003 that primarily provided clarification or enhanced consumer protections. To a lesser degree, some state regulators also reported that these changes imposed stricter licensing requirements on the various industry segments. State regulators views on the extent to which these changes strengthened their regulatory program varied, as shown in figure 4.

Figure 4: Extent to Which State Regulators Reported in 2011 That Statutory and Regulatory Changes Strengthened Their Regulatory Programs

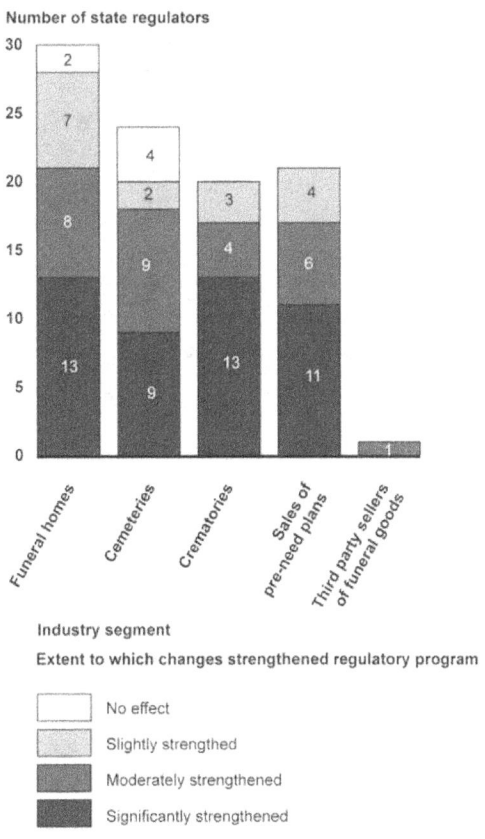

Number of state regulators

Industry segment

Extent to which changes strengthened regulatory program

- No effect
- Slightly strengthed
- Moderately strengthened
- Significantly strengthened

Source: GAO surveys of state regulators.

State regulators who responded to this issue on our 2011 survey reported that changes came about as a result of various factors, as shown in table 4.

Table 4: State Regulators' Views on Factors That Prompted Change in State Law or Regulation, as Reported in 2011

Industry segment	Accounts of desecration of human remains	Accounts of fraud or deceptive practices	Proposals from state regulatory agencies	Lobbying efforts of the death care industry	Lobbying efforts of consumer groups
Funeral homes	3	6	17	12	6
Cemeteries	5	9	16	10	6
Crematories	5	4	11	11	3
Sales of pre-need plans	0	15	16	7	6
Third party sellers of funeral goods	0	0	1	1	0

Source: GAO surveys of state regulators.

Note: Some state regulators also checked other in response to his question and these responses are not included in the table above.

Some of these changes, and the reason for these changes, were highlighted in our case study states, as shown below.

- Pursuant to a Colorado bill passed in 2009, funeral homes and crematories must now register with the state—prior to this, no such requirements existed. According to state regulators, this change came about as a result of lobbying efforts from the death care industry. Officials from a state association stated that the association sought out the regulation of the industry because although it believed that many reputable people operate the industry, a few bad individuals can give the entire industry a poor reputation.

- In Illinois, the Cemetery Oversight Act, passed in 2010, requires (1) the operators and other specified parties at nonexempt cemeteries to be licensed to operate in the state, (2) cemeteries to conspicuously display a consumer hotline number, and (3) cemeteries to file cemetery maps and enter burials and cremations into a state database.[61] According to state regulators, the bill was passed in response to an incident at an Illinois cemetery where graves were reported to be desecrated and vandalized in a scheme to resell burial plots to unsuspecting members of the public (see more on this incident in app. II).

---

[61] See 2009 Ill. Laws 863 (approved Jan. 19, 2010). As of November 2011, rules necessary to implement provisions of this act had not been implemented.

- An Oregon law passed in 2009 requires the licensure of death care consultants and the adoption of rules promoting environmentally sound death care practices.[62] According to state regulators, the statutory changes regarding the environmentally sound death care practices will help position them for future technological changes in the industry, such as alternative methods of final disposition.[63]

- In Tennessee, revisions to death care industry law and regulation in 2007 and 2008 included, among other things, requiring state or commissioner approval for a (1) change in trustee, (2) cemetery sale, and (3) pre-need contract. State regulators stated that these revisions were in reaction to a pre-need incident that involved the looting of about $20 million from pre-need trusts in Tennessee (see more on this incident in app. II).

- A Wisconsin law passed in 2008 brought more cemeteries under regulation. According to state regulators, as a result of this act, about 1,200 to 1,500 cemeteries fall under registration or licensing requirements, compared to 1991 when 5 cemeteries were required to be licensed. Officials also stated that the genesis for the legislative expansion was a general recognition by the state legislature that it was appropriate to have oversight of more cemeteries and that the effort to pass the law was spearheaded by a Wisconsin industry association.

See appendixes III through VII for more detailed information on the changes to state law and regulation in the five case study states. To view the survey covering funeral homes, funeral directors, and embalmers and the responding states' answers to the survey questions, go to GAO-12-91SP.

---

[62] Pursuant to Oregon law, a person practices as a death care consultant if the individual offers, for payment, consultations directly relating to the performance of a funeral or final disposition services. See Or. Rev. Stat. § 692.025(3).

[63] Alternative methods of final disposition may include such practices as alkaline hydrolysis, where a water-based chemical process is used to rapidly reduce a body to residue.

Views on Increasing Federal and State Regulation Varied

Views on Federal Regulation

State regulators' views on the need for the federal government to take a more active role in the regulation of the death care industry varied. State regulators who responded to this issue on our 2011 surveys frequently reported that they did not believe that there was a need for the federal government to take a more active role in regulating the death care industry; however, several also reported that they believe more federal involvement was needed, as shown in figure 5.[64]

---

[64] In some states, the same individual state regulator completed more than one of the surveys. The FTC promulgated the Funeral Rule in accordance with its authority to proh bit "unfair or deceptive acts or practices" and to prescr be "rules which define with specificity acts or practices which are unfair or deceptive acts or practices in or affecting commerce" and that such rules "may include requirements prescribed for the purpose of preventing such acts or practices." See 15 U.S.C. §§ 45(a)(1), 57a(1). GAO did not evaluate whether existing practices in the death care industry outside of the scope of the Funeral Rule fall within the scope of FTC's regulatory authority. If enacted, H.R. 900, the Bereaved Consumer's Bill of Rights Act of 2011, would grant FTC explicit authority to expand the scope of its regulation in the death care industry.

Figure 5: State Regulators' Views on the Need for the Federal Government to Take a More Active Role in Regulating the Death Care Industry, as Reported in 2011

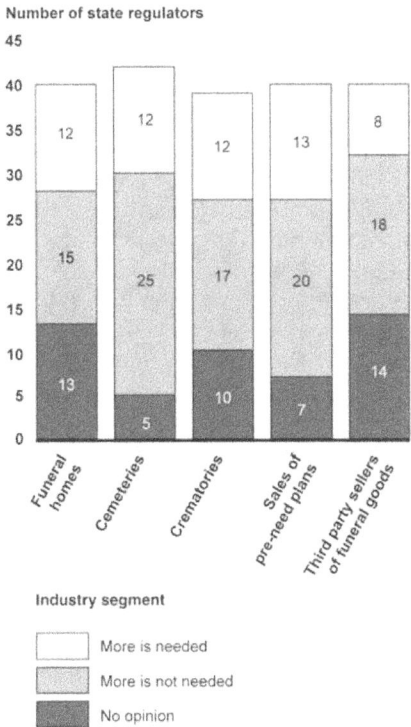

Number of state regulators

Industry segment

☐ More is needed

▢ More is not needed

▣ No opinion

Source: GAO surveys of state regulators.

State regulators who reported that they believe there was a need for the federal government to take a more active role in regulating the death care industry frequently stated that this was because minimum federal standards would help to provide uniformity across states.[65] Other reasons reported included (1) states do not have the resources to regulate the industry effectively and (2) minimum federal standards would help to prevent incidents or scandals from occurring. Of the state regulators who reported that they believe that there was not a need for the federal government to take a more active role in regulating the death care

---

[65] In some states, the same individual state regulator completed more than one of the surveys.

industry, they frequently reported that this was because the state is a better entity to regulate the industry. Other reasons reported included that current state or federal rules and regulations are sufficient.

The FTC and national associations' support of the Bereaved Consumer's Bill of Rights Act varied.[66] In a January 2010 statement, the Commission—which is headed by five FTC commissioners—testified that it supported the goals of the Bereaved Consumer's Bill of Rights Act which would extend the key consumer protections of the Funeral Rule to other segments of the death care industry, including cemeteries. In this statement, the Commission stated that an active enforcement program would be essential to ensure compliance with the requirements of the bill, as was the case with the Funeral Rule. FTC staff noted that although the number of cemeteries is unknown,[67] they anticipate that if the bill were enacted, it would likely double or triple the number of entities they have jurisdiction over. A 2010 report by the Congressional Budget Office states that based on information from the FTC, the agency would require five additional staff positions at a cost of about $1 million per year to develop and enforce the new requirements, train staff, and develop educational materials. The Congressional Budget Office estimates that implementing the legislation would cost the FTC about $5 million over a 5-year period.

Three of the six national associations we interviewed—including two industry associations and one consumer association—supported the Bereaved Consumer's Bill of Rights Act. However, officials representing two of the three associations that supported the bill stated that they were concerned that the proposed law would not require that all cemeteries be regulated. As one consumer association stated, "all grieving consumers are entitled to the same minimum protections." A fourth association—which represents state regulators—reported that it supported the existence of minimum standards and guidelines that could be established at the federal level, particularly since a comparable level of consumer protection does not exist in all states. However, this association also reported that the regulation of the death care industry should be done at

---

[66] As stated previously, this bill was introduced in 2011. However, a substantially similar bill had also been introduced in September 2009.

[67] Some states do not require cemeteries to register or require all types of cemeteries to be registered or licensed; as a result, the total number of cemeteries is not known. As stated previously, some states exempt religious, municipal, and family cemeteries from registration or licensing requirements.

the local level, and as such, the association reported that it would want an opt-out provision in the bill for states with an overall level of protection to consumers equal to or greater than that set forth in the Bereaved Consumer's Bill of Rights Act. Further, officials representing this association stated that if the bill is enacted, they are concerned that much of the work would be passed to the states. Finally, representatives from one industry association stated that it did not support the Bereaved Consumer's Bill of Rights Act for various reasons, including that it could impose excessive penalties for some relatively minor matters, such as fines of $16,000 for minor omission of consumer disclosures.[68]

Although the level of support for the Bereaved Consumer's Bill of Rights Act varied, officials representing four of the national associations, including some that supported the bill, stated that they believed the legislation would not ensure that incidents, such as the one that occurred at Burr Oak Cemetery—in which grave sites were reused—would be prevented from occurring in the future. According to documentation from one national association that represents state regulators, the association believes that it is unlikely that a federal system of examinations and investigations would discover such abusive conduct. The association document stated that absent a large appropriation of funds and more staff, the FTC would be severely challenged to establish a large enough footprint to be effective from an enforcement standpoint. This association further reported that it believes that enforcement is the key ingredient in protecting against inappropriate industry practices. Officials representing an industry association stated that they believe that the incidents that occurred at Burr Oak Cemetery involved actions that were already violations of state laws, and while laws and regulations can be enacted to provide consequences for violations, they do not prevent people from findings ways to violate the law or regulation. However, officials representing another industry association stated that they believed the Funeral Rule has dramatically improved the way funeral homes operate—making funeral homes more service oriented and resulting in no major incidents since the Rule was implemented, and if the Rule applied to other segments of the death care industry, these scandals possibly could be prevented.

---

[68] Officials we interviewed from one national association stated that their association had not issued a response to the Bereaved Consumer's Bill of Rights Act.

Views on State Regulation

State regulators reported facing some challenges to regulating the death care industry, and their views on the need for their state government to take a more active role in the regulation of the death care industry varied. In responding to our question about the biggest challenge they experience in regulating the death care industry, state regulators frequently reported that insufficient funds and/or staff to enforce regulations was the biggest challenge in enforcing the state's rules or regulations for each industry segment. However, when asked the degree to which this factor, as well as other factors, posed a challenge, state regulators reported varying views. For example, 18 of the 36 state regulators of funeral homes who responded to this issue reported that insufficient funds and/or staff was either not a challenge or a minor challenge, while 22 of the 36 state regulators of cemeteries who responded to this issue reported this factor was a major or moderate challenge.

State regulators views on whether they believe that there was a need for their state government to take a more active role in regulating the death care industry varied, as shown in figure 6.[69]

---

[69] In some states, the same individual state regulator completed more than one of the surveys.

Figure 6: State Regulators' Views on the Need for Their State Government to Take a More Active Role in Regulating the Death Care Industry, as Reported in 2011

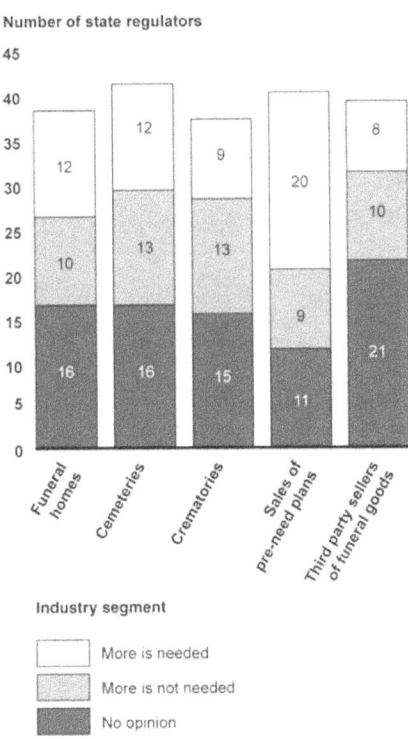

Number of state regulators

Industry segment

☐ More is needed

▨ More is not needed

▦ No opinion

Source: GAO surveys of state regulators.

State regulators from three of our case study states reported that their states had sufficient rules and regulations or were on the leading edge of regulation. Regulators from another state stated that they receive very few complaints against death care industry segments they regulate and as a result do not see the need for more regulation of such entities.[70]

---

[70] State regulators from the fifth state did not provide information on this issue.

GAO-12-65 Death Services

Agency Comments and Third-Party Views

We provided selected excerpts of the draft report to the FTC and the state regulators from our case study states to obtain their views and verify the accuracy of the information provided. We incorporated their technical comments into the report, as appropriate.

As agreed with your offices, unless you publicly announce the contents of this report earlier, we plan no further distribution until 30 days from the report date. At that time, we will send copies to the Federal Trade Commission and interested congressional committees. In addition, the report will be available at no charge on the GAO website at http://www.gao.gov.

If you or your staff have any questions about this report, please contact William O. Jenkins, Jr. at (202) 512-8777 or jenkinswo@gao.gov. Contact points for our Offices of Congressional Relations and Public Affairs may be found on the last page of this report. Key contributors to this report are list in appendix VIII.

William O. Jenkins, Jr.
Director, Homeland Security and Justice

Appendix I: Survey Methodology

To obtain information on the various ways states regulate the death care industry, how it has changed, and to what extent more regulation is needed we developed and administered five web-based surveys to all 50 states to provide current information on state regulation for each of the five death care industry segments—funeral homes, cemeteries, crematories, sales of pre-need funeral plans, and third party sellers of funeral goods. The surveys are similar to surveys we administered in 2003, and are designed to update and expand on information obtained in the earlier surveys. We surveyed state officials in all 50 states that were responsible for regulation or oversight of each of the death care industry segments and asked officials about current state laws and regulations, enforcement mechanisms, and consumer protections. We also solicited their views on the sufficiency of federal and state regulation.[1]

Survey development. A GAO social science survey specialist along with staff knowledgeable about the death care industry, including those who conducted work on two previous reports on the industry, developed the five survey instruments.[2] These surveys were primarily based on surveys that we developed and administered in 2003 for our work on the death care industry. We reviewed the engagement files from our 2003 work on the death care industry, including records of interviews, survey questions and results, and state regulator contact information—which provided a context and foundation for development of our current surveys. We also conducted interviews with officials at the Federal Trade Commission and six national associations to identify any additional issues to follow up on in the surveys.[3] In addition, we conducted a general news and journal literature search to identify emerging issues or trends we may want to address in the surveys.

---

[1] We did not include the District of Columbia in our 2003 survey, and as a result, did not include the District of Columbia in our 2011 survey either since we planned to compare survey responses from both years.

[2] GAO, *Funeral-Related Industries: Complaints and State Laws Vary, and FTC Could Better Manage the Funeral Rule*, GAO/GGD-99-156 (Washington, D.C.: Sept. 23, 1999), and *Death Care Industry: Regulation Varies across States and by Industry Segment*, GAO-03-757 (Washington, D.C.: Aug. 25, 2003).

[3] The six associations whose officials we interviewed included the Cremation Association of North America; National Funeral Directors Association; International Cemetery, Cremation, and Funeral Association; International Conference of Funeral Service Examining Boards; North American Death Care Regulators Association; and Funeral Consumers Alliance. A full description of our scope and methodology is included in the front of the report.

We conducted pretests of each of the five surveys in at least one state to ensure that the questions were clear and concise, and refined the instruments based on feedback we received as a result of the pretest. The bulk of the survey questions were taken from our 2003 survey and were pretested at that time. We wanted to keep many of the original questions without changing them in order to compare the results of the two surveys. In selecting the pretest states we identified several key criteria that guided our selection process. The criteria included (1) ensuring that the state regulates the segment of the industry that the survey addresses and (2) ensuring that the state has made regulatory changes since 2003—so that relevant questions would not be skipped during our pretests. We conducted pretests by phone with officials from Washington State to pretest the funeral home survey, Virginia for the cemetery survey, Kansas for the crematory survey, Mississippi and Louisiana for the sales of pre-need plans survey, and South Carolina for the third party sellers survey. We reviewed the entire survey with the pretest respondents, but focused on selected questions that were new or modified from our prior survey. The state regulatory officials responded to the questions asked, and we discussed any issues regarding clarity or understanding of the question. We made notes of the responses and any issues, and adjusted the questions as appropriate.

Identification of survey respondents. To develop an accurate e-mail contact list of state regulatory officials for each of the five segments of the death care industry for all 50 states, we used multiple sources. We started with a list of state regulators from the North American Death Care Regulators Association. We then compared this list to other lists we had obtained, adding additional detail. These other regulator contact lists included our 2003 survey contact list and lists from other national regulator, industry, and consumer associations, including the International Conference of Funeral Service Examining Boards, the Cremation Association of North America, and the Funeral Ethics Organization. We then used our consolidated list to contact, confirm, and update the list of state regulators who would receive our surveys. We contacted the individuals on this list by phone or e-mail to ensure that they were the proper contacts regarding regulation of the identified industry segment. We attempted to identify officials with direct responsibility for regulation. For some states, this meant we identified a number of different officials as survey recipients because some industry segments were regulated by different state entities. In other states, this meant we identified one official as the survey recipient for all five surveys in the state because one entity was responsible for regulation of all segments of the death care industry. However, if the state did not regulate a specific industry segment we sought out the office most appropriate to respond to our questions. In some states more than one entity regulated the same industry segment, and we selected an official from only one entity to respond to our survey. As such, we only collected information from one of the regulatory entities.[4]

Survey time frames and response rates. To ensure that we obtained the highest response rate possible, we made the web-based surveys available to the designated state contacts from April 14, 2011, through June 20, 2011.[5] We sent multiple reminders via e-mails and made telephone calls to the state officials requesting that they complete the surveys. Over this period, we obtained responses from 40 states covering regulation of funeral homes, 42 states covering regulation of cemeteries, 39 states covering regulation of crematories, 40 states covering regulation of sales of pre-need funeral plans, and 41 states covering regulation of third party sellers of funeral goods.[6] While the overall response rate was relatively high, not all states that completed the surveys provided responses to all the appropriate questions.

Many of the states that responded to our surveys in 2011 were the same states that responded in 2003. The response rate for all surveys in 2011 averaged about 81 percent, while the response rate for 2003 averaged about 90 percent. As shown in table 5, a high percentage of the states that responded to each of the segment surveys in 2011 also responded in 2003.[7]

---

[4] For example, in Maryland, two separate entities regulated sellers of pre-need plans— one regulates pre-need funeral plans and the other regulates pre-need cemetery plans. As stated by one of these regulators, different consumer protections may be available—such as a consumer protection account—depending upon which type of pre-need plan is being regulated. Further, each entity may be aware of complaints or violations received that the other entity is not. However, we could only send one survey to each state.

[5] Our surveys primarily asked state regulators to provide current information on the regulation of the industry. However, some questions asked regulators to provide data since 2003, some asked questions for data since 2008, and other questions asked about specific data for each year in 2008, 2009, and 2010.

[6] All but two states—Michigan and New Hampshire—responded to at least one of our five surveys.

[7] In addition, there were additional states that responded in 2003 that did not respond in 2011.

Table 5: Comparison of State Survey Respondents, 2003 and 2011

Industry segment	Number of states that responded in 2003	Response rate for 2003	Number of states that responded in 2011	Response rate for 2011	Number of states that responded in 2011 that also responded to 2003	Percentage of states that responded in 2011 that also responded to 2003
Funeral homes	48	96%	40	80%	39 of 40	98%
Cemeteries	44	88%	42	84%	38 of 42	90%
Crematories	45	90%	39	78%	35 of 39	90%
Sales of pre-need plans	42	84%	40	80%	34 of 40	85%
Third party sellers of funeral goods	45	90%	41	82%	38 of 41	93%

Source: GAO surveys of state regulators, 2003 and 2011.

Notes: All but two states—Michigan and New Hampshire—responded to at least one of our five surveys in 2011. All states except for Indiana responded to at least one of our surveys in 2003.

Survey analysis. In analyzing the five surveys, we computed descriptive statistics for all closed-ended survey questions, providing the frequency of specific responses as a proportion of the total number of states for which the question applied. We also developed a closed-ended question data run for each of our five case study states that completed an industry segment survey,[8] and we developed a close-ended data run for each question by state to be included in the e-supplement companion to the report. Open-ended survey responses were compiled for each of the five segment surveys and reviewed for content. In addition, open-ended responses for the most prevalent types of violations were compiled for all states that responded to the question. We also analyzed and compared the responses for survey data for selected questions to the responses we received in 2003. Differences in the responses from year to year could be attributable to the fact that different states responded in 2003 and 2011. Specifically, depending on the industry segment, 85 to 98 percent of those that responded to our 2011 survey also responded to our survey in 2003.

---

[8] The five case study states identified earlier in the report are Colorado, Illinois, Oregon, Tennessee, and Wisconsin.

Since this was not a sample survey, there are no sampling errors; however, the practical difficulties of conducting a survey may introduce errors, commonly referred to as nonsampling errors. For example, difficulties in interpreting a particular question, sources of information available to respondents, or entering data into a database or analyzing them can introduce unwanted variability into the survey results. We took steps in developing the questionnaires, collecting the data, and analyzing them to minimize such nonsampling errors. For example, as mentioned earlier, the surveys were developed by our survey specialist in collaboration with our staff with subject matter expertise. In addition, as stated earlier, we pretested the surveys with various states to ensure that the questions were clear and concise. Since this was a web-based survey, respondents entered their answers directly into the electronic questionnaire, eliminating the need to key data into a database, minimizing the opportunity for error. We examined the survey results and performed computer analyses to identify inconsistencies and other indications of error. An independent analyst checked the accuracy of all computer analyses. However, we did not independently verify the accuracy or completeness of the responses to the surveys.[9] This report does not contain all the results from the survey. The survey and a more complete tabulation of the results can be viewed at GAO-12-91SP. The special publication electronic supplement was created in accordance with the above described methodology to show the individual responses by state officials who replied to each of the questions on our five surveys.

We conducted this performance audit from October 2010 to December 2011 in accordance with generally accepted government auditing standards. Those standards require that we plan and perform the audit to obtain sufficient, appropriate evidence to provide a reasonable basis for our findings and conclusions based on our audit objectives. We believe that the evidence obtained provides a reasonable basis for our findings and conclusions based on our audit objectives.

---

[9] If state regulators provided responses to survey questions that they were instructed to skip or did not provide a response to a question that instructed them to go to the next question, such responses are not included in our analyses for this report and are not included in the e-supplement.

Appendix II: Pre-Need Plans, Consumer Education and Protection, and Allegations of Fraud and Mismanagement

Pre-Need Contracts for Funeral and Cemetery Arrangements

For the purposes of this report, a pre-need plan is defined as a contractual agreement whereby funeral arrangements, cemetery arrangements, or both are preplanned and prepaid for by an individual prior to his or her death.[1] Generally, the pre-need contract is between the individual for whom the services will be provided and the funeral director or cemetery operator. The options for paying pre-need expenses vary from state to state, and according to industry information and state regulators we contacted, the most commonly used options are trust accounts and insurance policies. Upon the individual's death, the representative of the funeral home or cemetery uses the trusted funds or the amount covered by the insurance policy to provide the designated goods and services.

- With an insurance-funded plan, generally the consumer purchases, either in a lump sum or by installments, an insurance policy that upon the consumer's death is paid out to provide the goods and services as specified in the contract.[2] These pre-need insurance policies typically have an increasing death benefit to cover future increases in the prices of funeral goods and services.

- With a trust-funded plan, the seller is generally required to deposit a certain percentage of the funds into a trust that is established in accordance with state law and managed by one or several trustees. State laws vary on how much of the pre-need funds must be placed into a trust, who can qualify as a trustee—such as a bank or other financial institution—and who receives any interest earned on a trust account.[3] The rationale behind this funding method is that interest earned on the trust account will accumulate over time and can be used to cover all or most of any increases in the cost of the goods and

---

[1] For our survey, we noted that the term "pre-need funeral plans" refers only to the purchase of funeral goods and services to be provided at a later date when the death of the individual for whom the purchase was made occurs. It does not refer to the purchase of a final expense insurance policy from which the beneficiary would claim and receive payment on the policy and be responsble for paying any costs for funeral goods and services on behalf of the deceased.

[2] Another option is to purchase an insurance annuity. Following the death of the purchaser, the annuity is paid out by the insurer to the death care provider to cover final expenses.

[3] The purchaser of the pre-need contract may be responsible for paying taxes on any trust account interest earned.

services purchased between the time the trust is established and the goods and services are provided, which may be a number of years.

According to state regulators from our five case study states, they have seen more insurance-funded pre-need contracts than trust-funded contracts in recent years. Pre-need insurance policies and trusts are generally regulated in accordance with state laws and regulations, which vary across states and set out specific requirements in terms of sales, licensing of sellers, and trusting or investing requirements. There is no uniform approach among states for regulating the pre-need industry.

Pre-need arrangements differ from funeral or cemetery arrangements made at the time of death (often referred to as "at-need" arrangements). Pre-need plans also differ from other methods a consumers may set up to cover some or all of their funeral or burial expenses, such as payable-on-death savings accounts and final expense insurance, which provide funds to pay funeral and cemetery expenses but in which the final disposition arrangements have not been made.[4] Another form of death care service is cemetery perpetual care, also called endowment care. This differs from pre-need plans in that it does not involve direct care of the individual at the time of death. Perpetual or endowment care refers to the general care and maintenance of developed portions of a cemetery and memorials or markers erected thereon and is financed from the income of an established trust fund.

Pre-need plans, and their associated contracts, may include a variety of differing provisions. Provisions can vary across states because of differing state laws and regulations, and by individual contract. Table 6 defines some of these provisions.

---

[4] For example, with a payable-on-death savings account, funds deposited by an individual remain available to that individual until his or her death, at which time the account becomes payable to a designated beneficiary, such as a funeral home or cemetery, for the purpose of covering funeral and related expenses. With a final expense insurance plan, the beneficiary would claim and receive payment on the policy and be responsible for paying any costs for funeral goods and services on behalf of the deceased. The beneficiary is generally not, however, legally bound to use the funds for their intended purpose. Typically, a spouse or close relative is the beneficiary of a final expense policy in order to carry out the policyholder's final wishes.

Table 6: General Definitions of Pre-Need Contract Provisions

Price-guaranteed and non-price-guaranteed	• Price-guaranteed goods and services refer to those items that are guaranteed for the price stated in the pre-need contract. Price guaranteed ensures that no additional funds are due at the time of death regardless of the actual cost of the goods and services at that time. • Non-price-guaranteed goods and services refer to those items where the price is not guaranteed in the pre-need contract. The contract holder may be required to pay additional funds at the time of death if the costs for the goods and services have increased.
Revocable and irrevocable	• A revocable pre-need contract is one which the consumer may cancel and the money paid is refundable. A cancellation fee may apply. • An irrevocable pre-need contract is one which the funds paid in are not refundable if the contract is canceled.
Portability or transferability	Portability or transferability refers to the ability of the consumer to move or transfer a pre-need contract, if at all, to another funeral or cemetery provider within the same state, or transfer to a provider in another state. Transfer limitations and fees may apply, and can vary among the states.
Trusting requirements	Trusting requirements include the amount of funds paid by the consumer for a trust-funded pre-need contract that the seller must deposit in a trust account. At the time of the consumer's death, the funds are to be used to pay for goods and services as specified in the pre-need contract. The percentage of funds that a seller must place in trust varies depending upon applicable state requirements. For example, Colorado law requires a seller to trust at least 75 percent of funds for funeral goods and services, while Oregon requires a seller to trust 90 percent for a guaranteed pre-need sale and 100 percent for a nonguaranteed pre-need sale.[a]

Source: GAO analysis based on death care-related documents from state regulators and associations.

[a]In addition, the amount of funds that a seller is required to trust can vary across the type of goods and services, depending on state law. For example, he Illinois law ultimately requires 95 percent trus ing of the purchase price for funeral services, personal property, and merchandise, but 85 percent trusting for the purchase price of outer burial containers. It further requires 50 percent trusting for cemetery goods and services. An official representing a na ional consumer association also pointed out hat some states do not require that all funds be retained in the trust account after initial deposit. For example, the association official explained that some states allow a percentage of trust funds (including 100 percent of all interest earned in some cases) to be withdrawn for administrative expenses.

Some industry associations have developed guidelines for pre-need laws that states can consider in developing their laws and regulations. Specifically, the National Funeral Directors Association and the International Cemetery, Cremation, and Funeral Association developed guidelines for pre-need statutes. However, according to one association's guidelines, the guidelines are not intended to provide states with exact statutory language or to be used in their entirety, but rather are intended to provide states with things to consider when developing requirements.[5] Furthermore, the National Association of Insurance Commissioners published model regulations for advertising life insurance and life insurance disclosures that also mention disclosure requirements for pre-need insurance. In addition, the association published a model regulation that discusses minimum standards for establishing reserve liability and nonforfeiture values.[6] However, this model regulation states that pre-need insurance is not well defined and recognizes that what constitutes pre-need insurance is subject to different interpretations by states. To view the survey covering pre-need plans and the responding states' answers to the survey questions regarding their state's laws and regulations, go to GAO-12-91SP.

Complete Data on Consumer Funds Invested in Pre-Need Contracts Are Not Available

Complete current data on the total funds invested in pre-need plans are not available. According to our survey of state regulators of pre-need plans, less than half of the state regulators responding (18 of 40) reported that they tracked the amount of funds invested in pre-need funeral plans. Of the 18 states reporting the tracking of pre-need funds, 9 provided data on the amount of funds invested in pre-need plans in their state, with amounts for all 9 states totaling $5.9 billion and amounts ranging from $1 million to $2.9 billion in each state. According to a 2011 study by a

---

[5] We do not have any basis to determine if these guidelines are appropriate or a best practice.

[6] A reserve liability may be described as an amount representing actual or potential liabilities kept by an insurer to cover debts to policyholders. According to the International Risk Management Institute, in a whole life insurance policy, the nonforfeiture value is defined as benefits that accrue to the insured when the policy lapses because of nonpayment of the premium.

death care industry consulting company, the estimated total dollars in pre-need accounts may have been nearly $35 billion in 2009.[7]

Federal and State Consumer Guides Help Educate and Protect Consumers

Since making funeral arrangements is often one of the most emotional experiences and expensive purchases a consumer will make, the FTC and some states have developed information to educate and help protect consumers. For example, FTC publishes a consumer guide that discusses some of the benefits of preplanning. Specifically, the guide states that

> "Thinking ahead can help you make informed and thoughtful decisions about funeral arrangements. It allows you to choose the specific items you want and need and compare the prices offered by several funeral providers. It also spares your survivors the stress of making these decisions under the pressure of time and strong emotions."

However, FTC's guide also states that

> "You may wish to make decisions about your arrangements in advance, but not pay for them in advance. Keep in mind that over time, prices may go up and businesses may close or change ownership. However, in some areas with increased competition, prices may go down over time. It's a good idea to review and revise your decisions every few years, and to make sure your family is aware of your wishes."

With regard to prepaying, FTC's guide goes on to say that

---

[7] Daniel M. Isard, *Funeral Preneed; In Force and Growth Over the Past Three Decades in the United States* (Phoenix: The Foresight Companies LLC, 2011).The report provides information on trust and insurance pre-need accounts, but does not include individually funded funeral arrangements such as personal life insurance, final expense life insurance or bank accounts marked "POD" or Paid on Death. The author of the study explained that there is no central depository for pre-need trust or insurance data, and that many companies consider this to be proprietary information. He said that his study represents an estimate done for economic understanding rather than a study of scientific measurement. He said that pre-need trust and insurance data had to be approximated to the nearest billion because banks and many state funeral associations keep their pre-need trust data confidential, and many insurance companies sell a variety of insurance and do not make their pre-need portfolios available. GAO was unable to determine the reliability of this report because data sources could not be identified and confirmed.

"Laws of individual states govern the prepayment of funeral goods and services;
various states have laws to help ensure that these advance payments are
available to pay for the funeral products and services when they're needed. But
protections vary widely from state to state, and some state laws offer little or no
effective protection."

FTC's guide also outlines some things consumers may want to consider
before entering into a pre-need contract. Specifically, FTC's guide states
that

"If you're thinking about prepaying for funeral goods and services, it's important
to consider these issues before putting down any money:

• What are you are paying for? Are you buying only merchandise, like a
casket and vault, or are you purchasing funeral services as well?

• What happens to the money you've prepaid? States have different
requirements for handling funds paid for prearranged funeral services.

• What happens to the interest income on money that is prepaid and put into a
trust account?

• Are you protected if the firm you dealt with goes out of business?

• Can you cancel the contract and get a full refund if you change your mind?

• What happens if you move to a different area or die while away from home?
Some prepaid funeral plans can be transferred, but often at an added cost."

Furthermore, FTC's guide suggests that a consumer tell their family about
the plans they have made and where the documents are filed. FTC
cautions that

"If your family isn't aware that you've made plans, your wishes may not be
carried out. And if family members don't know that you've prepaid the funeral
costs, they could end up paying for the same arrangements. You may wish to
consult an attorney on the best way to ensure that your wishes are followed."

States' guides provide similar educational information and cautions. For
example, a pamphlet published by an Oregon regulator discusses pre-
need planning and resources and notes that there are many honest and
reputable people and companies that offer pre-need funeral planning.
However, the pamphlet also cautions consumers to become educated
and obtain complete information on the laws and their rights because
"there are unscrupulous con artists who sell overpriced plans or will take
your money with no intention of fulfilling their promises." Likewise, a

Massachusetts consumer guide states that preplanning gives consumers the opportunity to shop around and the ability to designate their own preferences. The Massachusetts guide also provides a summary of consumer rights that are protected by law, and includes a checklist for pre-need funeral planning and arrangements. For example, Massachusetts informs consumers that if they wish to prepay for their funerals, the funeral director is to provide a standardized contract approved by the Board of Registration in Embalming and Funeral Directing, which includes an itemized statement of funeral goods and services that is FTC compliant, and a trust document with a bank or insurance policy. Funeral directors are also required to

- itemize all costs associated with the funeral and burial specifying those items where the cost is guaranteed and those items where the price may change,
- explain what will happen if they go out of business or if their funeral home is sold,
- disclose if they will receive a commission on the sale of an insurance policy, and
- provide written verification of where funds are being held if a trust account is used.

Massachusetts's checklist suggests that, when prearranging and prepaying for a funeral, consumers should

- use the standardized state contract,
- know which costs are guaranteed and which may change,
- know the name of the bank trustee if the contract is funded through a trust account or know the insurance company and policy number if the contract is funded through an insurance policy,
- know whether the funeral director received a commission if the contract is funded through an insurance policy,
- know what happens if the funeral home is sold or goes out of business,
- know whether and how the contract can be changed,
- know they have 10 days from signing to cancel the contract and get a refund, and
- notify a family member or legal representative of this arrangement.

California is an example of another state that has also developed a consumer guide—the Consumer Guide to Funeral and Cemetery Purchases. Like other states' guides, the California guide encourages pre-need planning and states that

> "Planning in advance for your own disposition after death can spare your loved ones the anguish of making difficult decisions while in a state of grief. Shopping ahead of time, getting correct information, and planning in advance allows you to make informed decisions before you purchase, and may save you money."

Also, like other states, the California guide discusses various aspects of pre-need insurance and trusts, and provides information to educate consumers what is allowable under California law. California's guide also advises consumers that they should visit and inspect several funeral establishments; and compare services restrictions, rules, and prices; and consider doing the following before they enter into a pre-need contract:

- ask for a guaranteed price plan and obtain a written estimate of any charges for any items or services that are not included in the plan,
- ensure that the contract includes a cancellation clause,
- ask if the funeral arrangements can be transferred to another funeral establishment, and
- find out where the money is being invested and who the trustees are.

Like Massachusetts' guide, California's guide suggests that consumers check the license status of a funeral provider, and provides links explaining key terms and required disclosures.

Allegations of Fraud and Mismanagement of Pre-Need Funds

The pre-need segment of the industry has also come under increasing scrutiny in recent years because of various allegations of fraud and mismanagement of pre-need funds. These allegations have arisen in various states across the country and involve the potential loss of millions of dollars in consumers' investments in pre-need trusts or insurance contracts. Some of these allegations involve criminal indictments for wire, bank, and mail fraud, and theft of pre-need deposits, while others involve civil litigation over the potential misappropriation of funds. Some of these allegations are currently pending either as criminal suits, civil suits, or both in various state and federal courts. The following are examples of reported incidents involving the sale of pre-need funeral and cemetery plans.

National Prearranged Services, Inc. In 2010, the U.S. Attorney for the Eastern District of Missouri filed a 50-count federal indictment against officials of National Prearranged Services, a Missouri-based company that sold prepaid funeral services. The indictment alleges fraud and other crimes for conduct spanning at least 35 states with approximate losses to purchasers, funeral homes, and state insurance guarantee associations ranging from $450 million to $600 million.[8] Missouri and Texas represent the two most affected states, where, according to media reports, 85,000 pre-need customers were affected. Charges alleged in the indictment included wire, bank, mail, and insurance fraud; money laundering; and multiple conspiracy charges involving the sale of pre-need funeral services. The violations allegedly took place from 1998 to 2008 and involved a number of illegal schemes. For example, the indictment alleged that officials withheld pre-need funds from trust and insurance accounts and removed funds from existing accounts for unauthorized purposes. The indictment also alleged that company employees used white-out or cross-outs to change the names of beneficiaries on pre-need insurance applications, including naming the company as sole beneficiary, in order to extract money without the customers' knowledge. Additionally, the indictment alleged that the defendants concealed their practices from insurance regulators. As a result of the various fraudulent schemes, the company and its associated entities were unable to meet their mounting obligations and collapsed in 2008. The case is ongoing in federal and various state courts.

Forest Hill. In 2007, the District Attorney General for Shelby County, Tennessee and the Commissioner of the Tennessee Department of Commerce and Insurance filed a complaint in Shelby County against the owners and other officials of Forest Hill Cemeteries and Funeral Homes seeking injunctive and other relief. Subsequently, according to a Shelby County District Attorney press release, Clayton Smart—an owner—and

---

[8] The case involves St. Louis-based National Prearranged Services, Inc, and affiliated entities including Texas-based companies Lincoln Memorial Life Insurance Company and Memorial Service Life Insurance Company. In a separate civil action, the National Organization of Life and Health Insurance Guaranty Associations is the plaintiff on behalf of the following state life and health insurance guaranty associations: Arizona, California, Colorado, the District of Columbia, Georgia, Idaho, Indiana, Iowa, Louisiana, Maryland, Michigan, Minnesota, Mississippi, Montana, Nebraska, Nevada, New Mexico, North Dakota, Ohio, Oregon, Rhode Island, South Dakota, Tennessee, Utah, Washington, West Virginia, Wisconsin, and Wyoming. Other plaintiffs include the state guaranty associations of Missouri, Texas, Illinois, Kansas, Oklahoma, Kentucky, and Arkansas.

others were indicted for violations in Tennessee that took place from 2004 to 2006, and that involved a number of illegal schemes, including money laundering by transferring stolen pre-need funds into accounts in the names of various corporations, entities, or investments owned or controlled by the defendants. According to the press release, the indictment also alleges that the transfers were under the guise of investing the funds for the benefit of the funeral home trusts and the beneficiaries of the prepaid funeral contracts, but in reality, the unauthorized transfers were for the defendants' benefit, as well as other individuals or relatives. The press release further states that as a result of these transfers, $20 million of the fund were lost. According to a 2010 Office of the Tennessee Attorney General annual report, Clayton Smart agreed to plead guilty to a charge of theft, as part of a global settlement with all the prosecuting jurisdictions. According to a Michigan Office of the Attorney General press release, Clayton Smart also pled guilty to counts of racketeering, embezzlement, and failing to properly trust or escrow funeral or cemetery or prepaid contract funds. The press release states that Clayton Smart embezzled up to $70 million in cemetery trust funds in Michigan. According to an official from the Tennessee Attorney General's office, the cases for two of the defendants are still pending.

Illinois Funeral Directors Association. In 2006, an audit by the Illinois Office of the Comptroller determined that the Illinois Funeral Directors Association's pre-need trust fund was in trouble and underfunded by nearly $40 million. According to the audit, the association, acting as a trustee for pre-need plans, collected unauthorized excess fees of approximately $9.6 million. At the time, the media reported that the trust fund was responsible for being able to pay for the contracted pre-need funerals of a reported 40,000 state residents at the time of need. State regulators told us that they are currently investigating why the trust fund was in trouble, and trying to figure out who was involved and what, if any, charges should be filed. As of June 2011, state regulators told us that no charges have been filed by the state. In 2009, class action lawsuits were filed by funeral directors who invested pre-need funds into the association's trust, alleging the fiscal mismanagement of the trust fund.[9] The funeral directors alleged that they lost more than $140 million, and that some funeral homes could go bankrupt because they have been

---

[9] According to media reports, the plaintiffs alleged that the trust operated as a Ponzi scheme where money from new purchasers of pre-need contracts was used to pay for the funerals of previous purchasers.

forced to pay the difference between what funerals actually cost and the inadequate amounts available from the trust fund.

The California Master Trust. In April 2011, the California Attorney General filed a complaint with the Superior Court of the State of California, County of Los Angeles against the California Master Trust, the California Funeral Directors Association, the Funeral Directors Service Corporation, and other defendants seeking a permanent injunction and restitution to consumers. According to a press release issued by the California Office of the Attorney General, the suit, which seeks to halt illegal activity and seeks restitution of about $14 million with interest, was filed on behalf of the Cemetery and Funeral Bureau of the Department of Consumer Affairs, which regulates the funeral industry in California. The suit was based on a June 2010 audit by the Cemetery and Funeral Bureau that alleges that millions of dollars of consumers' money paid to the trust was misspent or mismanaged, that defendants paid at least $4.6 million in illegal kickbacks to funeral homes, and that the defendants paid themselves excessive administrative fees.[10] According to the press release, the California Master Trust, which as of April 2011 controlled about $63.5 million, was created in 1985 by the funeral directors to pool the prepaid funeral payments of individual purchasers throughout California. The suit also seeks to wrest control of the trust away from the Funeral Directors Service Corp., a subsidiary of the California Funeral Directors Association, and place it under a new trustee, and seeks a full accounting of the trust's financial transactions as well as the defendants' financial transactions with the trust since 2000. Before this complaint was filed, the Funeral Directors Service Corporation, which served as the administrator of the California Master Trust, had filed a complaint in November 2010 with the Superior Court of the State of California, County of Sacramento, which contends, among other things, that the findings of the 2010 audit are incorrect. These cases are still pending in court.

One theme among these examples is that pre-need sellers were charged with or sued within the context of violating existing laws covering a variety of illegal activities that did not always focus on the state's laws or regulations governing pre-need plans. For example, the National Prearranged Services indictment cited charges for wire, bank, mail, and

---

[10] State of California, Department of Consumer Affairs, Cemetery and Funeral Bureau, *California Master Trust, Trustees, Comerica Bank & Funeral Directors Service Corp. Review for Compliance*, FD-07-03 (Sacramento: Revised June 2010).

insurance fraud; money laundering; and multiple conspiracy charges involving the sale of prepaid funeral services. The Clayton Smart indictment cited charges of failing to appropriately deposit funds collected, transferring funds to be used for unauthorized purposes, failing to submit accurate records, and money laundering. Many of the charges in these cases could apply to financial transactions associated with any business or industry. Nonetheless, officials from two states, Tennessee and Illinois, involved in the incidents described above told us that their states have made changes to existing laws as a result of the incidents that occurred in their respective states.

- In 2007 and 2008, the state of Tennessee conducted a major review and revision of its pre-need laws in reaction to the problems that occurred in the state. The officials said that in rewriting their laws, they wanted to be proactive and address any other future issues that potentially could arise. However, the officials told us that "morality cannot be legislated" as determined criminals will find a way carry out their actions. According to state regulators, Tennessee implemented a number of changes to strengthen its state death care laws, such as requiring state or commissioner approval, as applicable, for a change in trustee, cemetery sales, and pre-need contracts and for rollovers from trust funds to insurance. In addition, a pre-need cemetery consumer protection account was established in 2007, and a pre-need funeral consumer protection account was originally established in 2008.

- In 2010, legislation passed in the state of Illinois amended its pre-need laws as the result of concerns regarding the Illinois Funeral Directors Association's management of pre-need trust funds. Amendments enacted through the new legislation added a number of consumer protections. These included establishing a consumer protection fund for pre-need funeral plans, requiring an annual notice to all consumers regarding the status of their funds with an explanation of any fees charged by the trustee, clear identification of the trustee or insurance provider as well as the primary regulator of the trustee or insurance provider, and an explanation of the purchaser's right to a refund. In addition, all pre-need sales are

required to be entrusted with an independent trustee that is a
corporate fiduciary.[11]

[11] According to Illinois state regulators, prior to the new legislation funeral homes could act
as their own trustee if the fund was smaller than $500,000.

Appendix III: Colorado's Regulation of the Death Care Industry

Regulatory Structure	In Colorado, two state entities within the Department of Regulatory Agencies regulate some segments of the death care industry.

- The Office of Funeral Home and Crematory Registration regulates funeral homes and crematories. The office has two staff who spend a portion of their time on these death care-related areas.
- The Colorado Division of Insurance regulates pre-need contracts. Three staff in the office work on pre-need matters, as well as other insurance-related matters not related to the death care industry. These staff spend about 1/12th of their time on pre-need matters.

There are no state issued rules or regulations specific to cemeteries and third party sellers of funeral goods in Colorado.

Requirements and Enforcement Mechanisms

Funeral Homes, Funeral Directors, and Embalmers	**Licensing requirements.** Unlike in 2003 when the state regulator we surveyed reported that funeral homes are not regulated, as of 2010, funeral homes are required to be registered to operate in the state. Funeral directors or embalmers are required to practice at a registered funeral home but are not required to be registered with the state.[1] Funeral home applicants for registration are required to, among other things, (1) pay a registration fee, (2) provide a list of services provided at the funeral home, and (3) appoint an individual as designee of the funeral home. Funeral homes must renew their registration each year. According to the state regulator who responded to our 2011 survey on the regulation

---

[1] Although they are not required to be registered with the state, funeral directors are required to have at least 2,000 hours practicing or interning as a funeral director and have directed at least 50 services. Embalmers must have at least 4,000 hours practicing of interning as an embalmer and have embalmed at least 50 bodies. According to officials representing the Office of Funeral Home and Crematory Registration, the funeral home is responsible for ensuring that these individuals meet these requirements. Furthermore, according to an industry association, the association offers a voluntary certification program for practitioners, such as funeral directors, since the state of Colorado does not require individuals to be registered.

of funeral homes, there were approximately 187 funeral homes operating in Colorado.

Inspection and audit requirements. The state has the authority to investigate activities of a funeral home, but according to officials representing the Office of Funeral Home and Crematory Registration, such inspections are not conducted on a regular basis, as they are generally only done if there is a complaint made against a funeral home.

Consumer complaints and violations. According to the state regulator who responded to our 2011 survey on the regulation of funeral homes, the state received four consumer complaints regarding funeral homes in 2010, when it began regulating funeral homes, and identified four violations against funeral homes including ones related to unregistered practice, burying the wrong body, and refusal to release human remains until full payment was received. According to representatives from a Colorado industry association, they also receive consumer complaints and have received about 12 complaints in the last 3 years. Further, the state regulator who responded to this issue on our survey reported issuing two probations since 2008.

Cemeteries and Cemetery Operators

Cemeteries are not regulated at the state level. This was also the case in 2003 when we surveyed the Colorado state regulator of cemeteries.

Crematories and Crematory Operators

Licensing requirements. Unlike in 2003 when the state regulator we surveyed reported that crematories were not regulated, as of 2010, crematories are required to be registered to operate in the state. Crematory operators must practice at a registered crematory but do not have to be registered with the state.[2] Crematory applicants for registration are required to, among other things, (1) pay a registration fee, (2) provide a list of services provided at the crematory, and (3) appoint an individual as a designee of the crematory. Crematories must renew their registration

---

[2] Although not required to register with the state, a crematory operator is required to have at least 500 hundred hours practicing or interning as a crematory operator and have cremated at least 50 bodies. According to officials representing the Office of Funeral Home and Crematory Registration, the crematory is responsible for ensuring that these individuals meet these requirements. Furthermore, according to an industry association, the association offers a voluntary certification program for practitioners, such as crematory operators, since the state of Colorado does not require individuals to be registered.

every year. According to the state regulator who responded to our 2011 survey on the regulation of crematories, there were approximately 55 crematories operating in Colorado.

Inspections and audit requirements. The state has the authority to investigate activities of a crematory, but according to officials representing the Office of Funeral Home and Crematory Registration, inspections are not conducted on a regular basis, as they are generally only done if there is a complaint made against a crematory.

Consumer complaints and violations. According to the state regulator who responded to our 2011 survey on the regulation of crematories, the state received two consumer complaints regarding crematories in 2010, when it began regulating the crematories. In addition, the state regulator who responded to our survey reported that there were two violations, and reported that the violations typically involved crematories that were not registered. The state regulator who responded to our survey also reported that since 2008, the state had issued one letter of reprimand.

Cremation rate. According to the Cremation Association of North America, Colorado had a 63 percent cremation rate in 2009.[3]

Sales of Pre-Need Plans

Licensing requirements. Sellers of pre-need plans must be licensed to operate in the state. This was also the requirement in 2003, as reported by the state regulator who responded to our survey. Prospective licensees are required to, among other things, (1) pay an application fee and (2) provide documentation demonstrating a net worth of at least $10,000. According to the state regulator who responded to our survey, there were approximately 75 companies that sell pre-need plans—the majority of which are funeral homes, mortuaries, and cemeteries. Licensed pre-need sellers must renew their licenses once a year.

Inspection and audit requirements. The Colorado Division of Insurance has the authority to examine and investigate the pre-need contract seller to determine whether the pre-need contracts or forms of assignment comply with the seller's certification and Colorado law. According to

---

[3] These data are preliminary. As of September 2011, association officials stated that the data had not been finalized.

officials at the Colorado Division of Insurance, pre-need sellers are required to submit an annual report to them, and they review these annual reports to verify that the appropriate amount of money is in the trust and that money was properly funded. In addition, sellers are also required to keep records that the Colorado Division of Insurance is required to examine at least once every 5 years—a requirement that was implemented in 2010.[4]

Contract and trusting requirements. Various contract and trusting requirements exist in the state of Colorado.[5]

- Colorado permits both trust-funded and insurance-funded contracts. According to officials at the Colorado Division of Insurance, there are many more insurance-funded pre-need contracts in force in Colorado now than trust-funded contracts because of the rate of return, although the exact number was not provided. Contracts are required to be price guaranteed, and irrevocable and revocable contracts are both permitted.

- All pre-need contracts sold in Colorado must contain certain information and disclosures to assist consumers. Required information or disclosures include (1) a clear identification of the purchaser and the beneficiary, (2) a complete description of the goods and services purchased, and (3) the cancellation policy.

- Sellers are required to trust at least 75 percent of the sales of cemetery and funeral goods and services. A trustee must be a chartered state bank, savings and loan association, credit union, or trust company that is authorized to act as fiduciary and that is subject to supervision by the state bank or financial services commissioner or a national banking association, federal credit union, or federal savings and loan association authorized to act as fiduciary in Colorado.

---

[4] Pre-need sellers are required to pay for the examination that is conducted by contract examiners hired by the state. According to an industry association, the audit costs from $4,000 to $5,000 and is not structured in the most effective manner to identify fraud. The association officials stated that they are currently discussing these matters with the Colorado Division of Insurance.

[5] For more information on pre-need plans, see app. II.

- After the initial deposit of the funds into a trust—a minimum of 75 percent in Colorado—according to the state regulator who responded to our survey, only administrative fees can be withdrawn by a trustee.

- If a consumer cancels a contract, penalties may apply and the amount returned to the consumer may depend on when the cancellation is sought or the terms of the contract.

- Interest earned on a pre-need trust is the property of the contract seller, according to a consumer guide published by the Colorado Division of Insurance.

Consumer protection accounts. Colorado does not maintain a consumer protection account for pre-need contracts.

Funds invested in pre-need trusts. According to the state regulator who responded to our 2011 survey on the regulation of pre-need sales, Colorado does not track the amount of money invested in pre-need funds.

Consumer complaints and violations. According to the state regulator who responded to our 2011 survey on the regulation of pre-need plans, the Colorado Division of Insurance has taken four disciplinary actions against sellers of pre-need plans since 2008, reporting that the most prevalent violations included (1) unauthorized sellers, (2) failure to place funds into a trust, and (3) the use of pre-need contract forms that did not comply with law.

Incidents related to pre-need contracts have occurred since 2003 in Colorado.

- In one incident, a pre-need seller misled consumers and eluded Colorado's trusting requirements by offering consumers a pre-need plan that included two separate contracts—one for future services and another for the immediate purchase of goods. The seller trusted funds received for the future services contract but not for the goods contract. This issue was uncovered as a result of investigation by the Colorado Division of Insurance after two consumer complaints were filed with the division in 2008. The pre-need seller agreed to pay a fine for violations identified as a result of the investigation. Further, the seller agreed to trust 75 percent of the total sales of both contracts; requiring the seller to increase the amount of money trusted by about $1.5 million. According to officials representing a state industry association, although no consumers had been harmed in this situation, it was the largest amount of money involved in a pre-need incident in Colorado.

- In 2008, the Colorado Division of Insurance found that another seller did not properly trust funds from 23 pre-need contracts. The seller's license was suspended and the seller was ordered to trust the funds appropriately and pay a fine.

- In another case, a funeral home owner was selling pre-need contracts and not trusting any of the funds, even though the individual's license had been revoked. The Colorado Division of Insurance reported in 2006 that this incident was uncovered as a result of numerous consumer complaints received by the division. According to officials representing a state industry association, consumers lost all of their funds in this case, totaling about $500,000. The funeral home owner was fined.

According to officials representing the Colorado Division of Insurance, the division is limited in the amount of authority it has to take punitive actions. The division's administrative sanctions include a $1,000 fine per incident and the suspension or removal of a practitioner's license. However, officials stated that they can refer violators to other agencies, such as the local district attorney for criminal prosecution.

| Third Party Sellers of Funeral Goods | A person who sells caskets, urns, or other funeral goods but does not provide funeral services is exempt from any requirements in the Colorado Mortuary Science Code. |

Legislative Changes and Rationale

State regulatory officials reported various changes to state laws and regulations regarding the death care industry since 2003. As reported by Colorado state regulators who responded to our 2011 surveys, changes included those that clarified legislation or regulation, enhanced consumer protections, changed the state's regulatory organization, and imposed stricter licensing requirements. Respondents stated that they believe these changes either slightly or significantly strengthened their regulatory program. Specific examples of these changes are listed below.

- Pursuant to legislation passed in 2009, funeral homes and
  crematories are now required to be registered with the state.[6]
  According to state regulators, this change came about as a result of
  lobbying efforts from the death care industry. Officials from a state
  association stated that the association sought the regulation of the
  industry because although it believed that many reputable people
  operate the industry, a few bad individuals can give the entire industry
  a poor reputation.

- Legislation passed in 2010 authorizes the Colorado Department of
  Insurance to use independent contractors to review the contracts from
  all sellers once every 5 years. According to an official from the
  department, a 2009 sunset review of legislation recommended
  requiring these examinations of pre-need contracts because of some
  improprieties of pre-need sellers that had taken place at the time. This
  official further stated that other than this new requirement, the state
  statute regarding pre-need has remained largely unchanged since the
  original 1995 legislation.

- In April 2011, a law was passed to ensure that alternative methods of
  cremations, such as alkaline hydrolysis, also fall under the cremation
  regulations.[7]

---

[6] According to officials representing the Office of Funeral Home and Crematory
Registration, under current law, one registered facility where bodies are prepared could be
registered, but services could be performed at various facilities that do not have to be
registered. Officials stated that there is a proposed bill that if enacted would ensure that all
facilities are required to be registered individually.

[7] According to officials from the Cremation Association of North America, alkaline
hydrolysis is a water-based chemical process that is used to reduce a body to residue.

Appendix IV: Illinois's Regulation of the Death Care Industry

Regulatory Structure

In Illinois, two state entities directly regulate the death care industry. Some regulatory responsibilities may transition between the two entities under legislative changes that are being made.

- The Illinois Department of Financial and Professional Regulation has regulatory responsibility for funeral directors, embalmers, and cemetery operators. The department has eight total staff and three investigators. Depending upon how the recently enacted Cemetery Oversight Act is ultimately implemented, additional staff may be added to help with the oversight of cemetery operators. Staff have responsibilities other than dealing with death care-related matters. In addition, two boards within the also assist with regulation. The Funeral Directors and Embalmers Licensing and Disciplinary Board provides advice and recommendations to the department staff upon request regarding rulemaking and disciplinary decisions. The board is made up of seven members appointed by the Secretary—this should include six licensed funeral directors and embalmers, and one public member. The Cemetery Oversight Board consists of the Secretary of the Illinois Department of Financial and Professional Regulation, who serves as chairperson, and eight members appointed by the Secretary; the eight members must include five members who represent segments of the cemetery industry, two members who represent consumer interests, and one member who represents the interests of the general public.

- The Illinois Office of the Comptroller regulates sales of pre-need plans and crematory operators. The office is authorized 10 staff positions and 10 field auditor positions.

According to the state regulator who responded to our survey on the third party sellers of funeral goods, there are no rules or regulations specific to third party sellers of funeral goods in Illinois.

Requirements and Enforcement Mechanisms

Funeral Homes, Funeral Directors, and Embalmers

Licensing requirements. Funeral homes are not regulated, but funeral directors and embalmers are required to be licensed to operate in the state. This was also the case in 2003 when we surveyed the Illinois state regulator. Illinois offers a joint license for funeral directors and embalmers. Prospective licensees are required to, among other things, (1) pay an application fee, (2) be at least 18 years of age, (3) complete an internship of at least 1 year under a licensed funeral director or embalmer, (4) pass the requisite exam, (5) complete 30 semester hours of college credit, and (6) have an associate's or baccalaureate degree in mortuary science from an approved program of mortuary science or an equivalent associate's degree. Funeral directors and embalmers must renew their joint license every 2 years as well as complete 24 hours of continuing education within a 24-month period. In June 2011, Illinois Department of Financial and Professional Regulation officials reported that there were 2,794 funeral directors and embalmers licensed in Illinois.[1]

Inspection and audit requirements. The Illinois Department of Financial and Professional Regulation has the authority to conduct inspections and audits. According to department officials, the department has audited funeral homes in the past but has not done so recently because of resource constraints. During these prior audits, officials stated that they would contact staff at a sample of funeral homes and ask them to produce certain information, such as continuing education records, and in some cases, officials visited funeral homes in person.

Consumer complaints and violations. Consumer complaints regarding funeral homes and funeral directors are collected by various entities in Illinois.

- According to the 2009 Cemetery Oversight Task Force report, the Illinois Attorney General receives about 70 complaints each year for cemeteries, funeral homes, and monument companies.[2] According to the Attorney General, complaints against funeral homes were often based on the failure of the funeral homes to provide promised services, the quality of the products or services, or confusion about the cost of services.

---

[1] In addition to the joint licensees, officials reported that there were 142 licensed interns and 89 funeral director licensees—the latter of which were issued prior to the state offering the joint license.

[2] In 2008, the Illinois Attorney General received a total of 33,335 consumer complaints.

- An official from one industry association stated that it receives about one to two complaints each week. According to this association, it will attempt to resolve the matter if it involves one of its members, and about 75 percent of the time the association is able to do so. Most complaints the association receives are related to a consumer who is unhappy with a service received from a funeral director, but on occasion the association will also get complaints in which consumers claim that they paid for something but did not receive it.

- Another industry association reported that from January 2002 to June 2011 it had received 305 complaints or inquiries regarding the industry. Complaints consisted of concerns about maintenance, contractual obligations, customer service, business conduct, and general questions. According to officials, the association will intervene on behalf of the consumer regarding complaints against the industry and attempt to resolve these issues.

From January 2011 to June 2011, the Illinois Department of Financial and Professional Regulation took disciplinary actions against 11 different funeral directors or embalmers. Specifically, the department took action on 4 of these licensees because they defaulted on an educational loan or did not pay their state taxes, issued cease and desist orders against two funeral directors who were unlicensed, and reprimanded and fined another for failure to implement sufficient protocols to prevent misidentification of cremated human remains. For the remaining 4, the Illinois Department of Financial and Professional Regulation either placed them on probation or revoked their licenses for actions that included violation of regulations, unprofessional conduct, or untrustworthiness.

Cemeteries and Cemetery Operators

Licensing requirements. Licensing requirements for cemetery operators have changed since we surveyed state regulators in 2003. According to officials representing the Illinois Office of Financial and Professional Regulation, in 2003, cemetery operators had to be audited if their cemetery had a care fund of more than $250,000, and licensed if they were selling pre-need plans and were not exempt.[3] This requirement

---

[3] According to the state regulator who responded to our survey in 2003, the types of cemeteries that were exempt from regulation at the time included fraternal, municipal, state, federal, religious, and family cemeteries. Regardless of whether a cemetery maintains a care fund or sells pre-need plans, every cemetery is required to register with the Illinois Office of the Comptroller.

remained the same until passage of the Cemetery Oversight Act in 2010, which requires cemetery operators and customer service personnel to be licensed to operate in the state. However, according to officials from the Illinois Department of Financial and Professional Regulation, since rules implementing applicable provisions of the act have not been approved as of November 2011 and because trailer bills are being discussed that would change the act, not all requirements under the act have been implemented. As presently enacted, the act exempts or partially exempts some cemeteries from its requirements.

- Cemetery operators of family burial grounds; cemetery operators that have not engaged in any interments, inurnments, or entombments in the last 10 years and do not accept or maintain care funds; and cemeteries that are smaller than 2 acres and that do not accept or maintain care funds are fully exempt from requirements of the act.

- Cemetery operators of public cemeteries, religious cemeteries, and cemeteries with 25 or fewer interments, inurnments, or entombments in the prior 2 years that do not accept or maintain care funds may apply for partial exemption from requirements of the act.[4]

Under the act, to become a cemetery operator (referred to as a cemetery authority in the act), prospective licensees must, among other things, (1) pay an application fee, (2) establish that he or she is of good moral character, and (3) provide evidence that the applicant has financial resources to comply with maintenance and record-keeping provisions of the act. Prospective licensees for positions of cemetery manager or customer service employee at a licensed cemetery must, among other things, (1) pay an application fee, (2) be at least 18 years of age, (3) complete a high school education or an equivalent, and (4) pass the requisite exam. The act further provides that license expiration, renewal, and other requirements, which have yet to be implemented. According to an official from the Illinois Department of Financial and Professional Regulation, Illinois does not have current data on the number of cemeteries that operate in the state, but will as a result of the Cemetery Oversight Act.

---

[4] Operators of partially exempt cemeteries are not required to be licensed, but must meet other requirements such as filing and maintaining a map of the cemetery; entering the number of interments, inurnments, or entombments into the department's database; and adhering to the consumer bill of rights.

Inspection and audit requirements. The Illinois Department of Financial and Professional Regulation has the authority to conduct inspections and audits. In addition, the Cemetery Oversight Act requires that all cemeteries subject to the act submit an annual report to the department, subject to any rules of the department specifying the contents of the required reports.

Under the Cemetery Oversight Act, cemeteries are required to keep various records.

- Cemeteries are required to record burials and cremations in the Illinois Department of Financial and Professional Regulation's Cemetery Oversight Database. From December 2010 to June 2011, 1,037 cemeteries entered 23,290 burials into the database. The Illinois Department of Financial and Professional Regulation estimates that this is about 75 percent of all required burial entries. According to one industry association, although some cemetery operators of smaller cemeteries were initially concerned that the database would be burdensome, once it was implemented, many operators reported the usefulness of having digital records as a result of the new database.

- Cemetery operators are required to maintain a cemetery map, detailing items such as the location of all plots.

- Cemeteries are required to provide consumers with a price list for all cemetery products offered for sale.

Consumer complaints and violations. Consumer complaints regarding cemeteries or cemetery operators are collected by various entities in Illinois.

- As stated previously, the Illinois Attorney General receives about 70 complaints each year regarding cemeteries, funeral homes, and monument companies. The most frequent complaints they receive calls about are regarding cemetery maintenance—such as the upkeep of gravesites—and issues with respect to pre-need contracts.

- According to officials representing the Illinois Department of Financial and Professional Regulation, the department's consumer hotline has been in effect since March 2010, and they have received just over 175 calls as of December 2010, but more than half of the calls were not complaints. Of the calls received, 84 were complaints—about 50 of which were related to maintenance and about 30 were related to memorial or marker issues. According to the state regulator who responded to our 2011 survey on the regulation of cemeteries, the complaint hot-lines are one of the state's most effective consumer protections.

- As stated previously, an Illinois industry association reported that from January 2002 to June 2011 it had received 305 complaints or inquiries regarding cemeteries and funeral homes. Complaints consisted of concerns about maintenance, contractual obligations, customer service, business conduct, and general questions.

Crematories and Crematory Operators

Licensing requirements. Crematory operators are required to be licensed to operate in the state. Prospective licensees are required to, among other things, (1) pay an application fee and (2) obtain a certification from an approved training program for all employees who will operate the cremation unit. There are no requirements for crematory operators to renew their licenses. In June 2011, the Illinois Office of the Comptroller reported that there were 102 licensed crematory operators.

Inspections and audit requirements. The Illinois Office of the Comptroller has the authority to conduct inspections and audits.[5] In addition, each crematory operator is required to file an annual report with the Illinois Office of the Comptroller.[6] The report must, among other things, provide the total number of cremations performed at the crematory in the prior year and include an attestation by the licensee that all applicable permits and certifications are valid.

Consumer complaints and violations. According to the state regulator who responded to our 2011 survey, no consumer complaints regarding crematories were received in 2008, 2009, and 2010 and no violations against crematories or crematory operators were reported since 2008.

---

[5] Effective March 12, 2012, the Department of Financial and Professional Regulation is the authority responsible for conducting such inspections.

[6] Effective March 12, 2012, such annual reports are to be filed with the Department of Financial and Professional Regulation.

Cremation rate. According to the Cremation Association of North
America, Illinois had a 34 percent cremation rate in 2009.[7]

Sales of Pre-Need Plans

Licensing requirements. Sellers of pre-need plans are required to be
licensed to operate in the state. Prospective licensees are required to,
among other things, (1) pay an application fee and (2) provide a detailed
statement of their assets and liabilities. Further, according to the state
regulator who responded to our survey, a licensee must be associated
with a licensed funeral home or cemetery. There are no requirements that
pre-need sellers renew their licenses. As of June 2011, the Illinois Office
of the Comptroller reported that there were 1,042 pre-need sellers
licensed in the state.

Inspection and audit requirements. The Illinois Office of the
Comptroller has the authority to conduct inspections and audits and
examine any books or records related to a pre-need licensee. According
to officials representing the Illinois Office of the Comptroller, they try to
audit pre-need sellers every 4 to 5 years. Given limited resources,
officials stated that they try to focus on those businesses with the largest
amount of money invested in pre-need. In addition, licensees must file an
annual report with the Illinois Office of the Comptroller. According to
officials representing the office, they review these annual reports,
examining the financial information in the reports to ensure that funds
have been properly trusted and there is no abnormal fluctuation from
beginning to end of year data.

Contract and trusting requirements. Various contract and trusting
requirements exist in the state of Illinois.[8]

- Insurance-funded and trust-funded pre-need contracts are permitted
  in Illinois. According to officials representing the Illinois Office of the
  Comptroller, funeral homes began to move from more trust-funded
  plans to more insurance-funded plans. They explained that from the
  consumer's standpoint, consumers who purchase insurance-funded
  plans are more in control of their funds and such plans are less risky.

---

[7] These data are preliminary. As of September 2011, association officials stated that the
data had not been finalized.

[8] For more information on pre-need plans, see app. II.

According to the state regulator who responded to our 2011 survey, irrevocable, revocable, guaranteed, and nonguaranteed pre-need contracts are all permitted in Illinois. However, pre-need cemetery plans must be sold on a guaranteed price basis.

- All pre-need contracts sold in Illinois must contain certain information and disclosures to assist consumers. Required information or disclosures include (1) a clear identification of the purchaser and the beneficiary, (2) a complete description of the goods and services purchased, and (3) the cancellation policy.

- Sellers are required to trust 85 percent of the purchase price of outer burial containers; 95 percent of the purchase price of funeral services, personal property, and merchandise; and 50 percent of all cemetery goods and service sales, except outer burial containers (of which 85 percent must be trusted), with a corporate fiduciary.

- A trustee is generally allowed to withdraw a reasonable fee. In addition, a trustee is required to annually furnish to each purchaser a statement identifying (1) the receipts, disbursements, and inventory of the trust, including an explanation of any fees or expenses charged by the trustee; (2) an explanation of the purchaser's right to a refund, if any; and (3) the primary regulator of the trust as a corporate fiduciary under state or federal law.

- With respect to a pre-need cemetery sale, if a seller changes trustees, the trustee must provide written notice of the change to the Comptroller no less than 28 days prior to the change in trustee.

- According to the state regulator who responded to our survey, consumers can transfer or cancel their contracts but penalties may apply. According to an Illinois Funeral Directors Association guide, unless a contract is made irrevocable, a consumer may cancel a pre-need contract at any time. The penalties for canceling a pre-need contract will be different depending upon when the contract is canceled.

- According to officials from the Illinois Office of the Comptroller, if money is left over in a trust fund for guaranteed contracts, the money should go to the estate. However, if the contract is nonguaranteed, there is no applicable requirement.

Consumer protection accounts. Illinois has two consumer protection accounts—one for pre-need cemetery plans and another for pre-need

funeral plans. The cemetery account was created in 1986 and the funeral
account in 2010. For each pre-need contract sold, sellers must contribute
$5 to the respective account. Funds from these accounts are to be used
for consumer restitution. According to officials representing the Illinois
Office of the Comptroller, in June 2011, no claims have been made for
the funds from the funeral account but the cemetery account was utilized
in 2010, although prior to this use, the account had not been used in
about 10 years.

Funds invested in pre-need trusts. As of June 2011, the Illinois Office
of the Comptroller reported that there was over $300 million held in trusts
for pre-need funeral plans, over $1.4 billion held in insurance for pre-need
funeral plans, and over $71 million held in pre-need merchandise funds.

Consumer complaints and violations. Consumer complaints regarding
pre-need sellers are collected by various entities in Illinois. According to
the state regulator who responded to our 2011 survey on the regulation of
pre-need plans, the state had received about 27 consumer complaints
regarding pre-need plans in 2008, 46 in 2009, and 21 in 2010. Officials
representing the Illinois Office of the Comptroller stated that the common
types of complaints received included those related to contract disputes
and refund delays. Further, these officials stated that a newer complaint
that they are starting to receive is related to pre-need plans that are
funded by extended life insurance policies, and that in these cases,
consumers are paying a lower monthly payment for a limited time period
at the end of which they are to pay the entire remaining balance. If
consumers are unable to pay the remaining balance, they are required to
continue to make payments but end up paying significantly more than
their purchase is worth. Officials stated that they are looking into this
issue to determine if there is any violation of the law.

According to the state regulator who responded to our 2011 survey on the
regulation of pre-need plans, there were approximately 100 violations
against licensees for pre-need sales since 2008. The top three most
prevalent types of violations noted by the state regulator who responded
to this issue were (1) improper entrustment of funds, (2) improper
fiduciary oversight of funds or improper withdrawal, and (3) contract
language failing to meet statutory requirements. Officials representing the
Illinois Office of the Comptroller stated that they are very limited on the
types of disciplinary actions that they can take against licensees. For
example, to revoke or suspend a license, the process is slow and the
proceedings are very costly. Officials compared this to other states where

if a licensee doesn't file the appropriate information, then the license is automatically suspended.

Officials noted that they believe that one of the benefits of the Cemetery Oversight Act is that between the Illinois Department of Financial and Professional Regulation and the Illinois Office of the Comptroller, the state will likely be able to take more actions. Illinois Office of the Comptroller officials also stated that they would like to have a licensee lookup system similar to the one the Illinois Department of Financial and Professional Regulation has for its funeral director and embalmer licensees—which is available for public use. The Illinois Office of the Comptroller is discussing doing this but needs to define terms, such as what is considered a significant issue.

Third Party Sellers of Funeral Goods

According to the state regulator who responded to our 2011 survey on the regulation of pre-need plans, other than rules or regulations that generally apply to all businesses, Illinois does not have rules or regulations in place that specifically address third party sellers of funeral goods.

Legislative Changes and Rationale

State regulatory officials reported various changes to state laws and regulations regarding the death care industry. As reported by the state regulators who responded to our 2011 surveys, changes included those that enhanced consumer protections, provided clarification of legislation or regulation, changed the state's regulatory organization, and imposed stricter licensing requirements, and that these changes either slightly or significantly strengthened the state's regulatory program. Specific examples of these changes include the passage of the Cemetery Oversight Act and amending the Illinois Funeral or Burial Funds Act.

- The Cemetery Oversight Act was passed in 2010 in response to a reported incident at an Illinois cemetery and to address task force recommendations, as indicated by officials from the Illinois Department of Financial and Professional Regulation. Workers at an Illinois cemetery were reported to have desecrated and vandalized graves in a scheme to resell burial plots to unsuspecting members of the public. As a result of these allegations, the Governor created the Cemetery Oversight Taskforce to review the incident and make recommendations. The task force concluded that among other things, the lack of regulatory oversight was a contributing factor to the criminal scheme that occurred at the cemetery. Recommendations made by the taskforce included the following: (1) consolidate the regulatory authority of funeral and burial practices to the Illinois Department of Financial and Professional Regulation, (2) consider the adoption of new legislation that provides for the licensure of cemetery managers and ensure that only qualified persons are authorized to own or operate a cemetery, and (3) consolidate and amend existing statutes. Among other things, the Cemetery Oversight Act requires certain cemetery operators to be licensed to operate in the state,[9] requires that cemeteries conspicuously display the department's consumer hotline number, requires cemeteries to file cemetery maps, and requires cemeteries to enter burials and cremations into a database developed by the Illinois Department of Financial and Professional Regulation.

According to officials from the Illinois Department of Financial and Professional Regulation, because of concerns about the costs to cemeteries in meeting requirements under the Cemetery Oversight Act, particularly smaller cemeteries, no rules have been issued as of November 2011. According to one Illinois industry association, the association supported the act despite knowing that there were concerns and more work would need to be done before the act was fully implemented. An official representing this association stated that, as a result of the incident at the Illinois cemetery, the political climate demanded that some legislation be passed. According to another industry association, laws were already in place, prior to the Cemetery Oversight Act that addressed conduct that occurred at this cemetery. The Illinois Department of Commerce and Economic Opportunity analyzed the potential impact of the Cemetery Oversight Act and agreed that the act would have a significant impact on approximately 119 small businesses.[10] According to officials from the Illinois Department of Financial and Professional Regulation, trailer bills have since been introduced to address the concerns related to the act.

---

[9] Specifically, it requires the operators and other specified parties at nonexempt cemeteries to be licensed to operate in the state.

[10] Specifically, the report stated that (1) fully regulated cemeteries will have a minimum additional cost of about $127 per burial; (2) partially exempt cemeteries will incur a minimum additional cost of about $34 per burial; (3) the industry believes that in some cases, it could cost as much as $10,000 per year to be in compliance with licensing, legal fees, fines, accounting fees, and additional staff; (4) the act will have a significant impact on approximately 119 small businesses; and (5) none of the small businesses affected gross more than $4 million per year.

- The Illinois Funeral or Burial Funds Act was amended in 2010 in response to the concerns regarding an Illinois association's management of pre-need funds (see more on this issue in app. II). The new law, among other things, (1) established a consumer protection fund for pre-need funeral contracts and (2) required that all pre-need sales be entrusted with a corporate fiduciary that is independent.

Although the state regulators reported that changes such as the Cemetery Oversight Act and the amendments to the Illinois Funeral or Burial Funds Act have strengthened Illinois's regulatory program, some state association representatives in Illinois stated that they believe that these laws would not have prevented incidents similar to those that occurred at the Illinois cemetery or with the funeral association trust. State regulators state that there is no way to be sure if the changes to the laws would have prevented these kinds of incidents, but that there may have been the ability them earlier. Further, state regulators in Illinois stressed the importance of consumer education and whistleblower protections to help prevent and detect future problems.

Appendix V: Oregon's Regulation of the Death Care Industry

Regulatory Structure

In Oregon, two entities regulate the death care industry.

- The Oregon Mortuary and Cemetery Board is responsible for regulation of funeral homes, funeral directors, embalmers, cemeteries, crematories, and salespersons of trust-funded pre-need plans, among others. The board is made up of 11 members who are appointed by the Governor. Three members are required to be representatives of cemeteries, 2 members must be licensed funeral service practitioners, 1 must be a licensed embalmer, 1 must be a representative of a crematory, and 4 must be public representatives. In addition, the Oregon Mortuary and Cemetery Board has 5.71 full-time equivalent staff, including one full-time inspector and one full-time investigator.

- The Division of Finance and Corporate Securities within the Department of Consumer and Business Services has regulatory responsibilities for pre-need trust accounts. The Department of Consumer and Business Services has a 0.8 full-time equivalent staff for registration, examination, and regulation of pre-need trusts and contracts.

There are no rules or regulations specific to third party sellers of funeral goods in Oregon.

Requirements and Enforcement Mechanisms

Funeral Homes, Funeral Directors, and Embalmers

Licensing requirements. Funeral homes, funeral directors, and embalmers must be licensed to operate in the state, which was also was the case in 2003, as reported by the Oregon state regulator responding to our survey. Funeral home applicants must, among other things, (1) pay a fee and (2) disclose that the home will be operated by licensed funeral service practitioner. Prospective funeral director and embalmer licensees are required to, among other things, (1) pay a fee, (2) pass an exam, and (3) have 1 year of prior experience. Embalmers licensees must have also graduated from an accredited program of funeral service education, and funeral service practitioners must generally have graduated from an appropriate associate's degree program. Funeral home, funeral director, and embalmer licensees are required to renew their licenses every 2 years. According to the state regulator responding to our 2011 survey on the regulation of funeral homes, there were approximately 200 funeral homes operating in Oregon.

Inspection and audit requirements. The Oregon Mortuary and Cemetery Board is required to inspect funeral homes every 2 years, but may also conduct random inspections at other times. In conducting inspections, the board utilizes a standard funeral establishment inspection checklist. According to an official representing the board, items on the checklist include (1) sanitation of the facility, (2) whether the facility's license is posted, (3) whether price lists are available and contain required disclosures and no misrepresentations and (4) the accuracy and completeness of arrangement records. According to officials representing the Oregon Mortuary and Cemetery Board, resources are not available to do many on-site inspections.

Consumer complaints and violations. According to the state regulator responding to our 2011 survey on the regulation of funeral homes, the state received approximately 60 complaints in 2008, 45 in 2009, and 43 in 2010.

According to an official from the Oregon Mortuary and Cemetery Board, the typical complaints received regarding funeral homes involve (1) overcharging; (2) inappropriate conduct, such as being rude; (3) unlicensed activity; and (4) misrepresentation, such as telling consumers something is required when it is not or advertising that they have the lowest prices when they do not. As a result of complaints, applications, or inspections, an official from the Oregon Mortuary and Cemetery Board reported that the board had 105 cases opened against funeral homes over a 3-year period—2008, 2009, and 2010.[1] Further, the state regulator who responded to this issue on our survey reported taking various enforcement actions since 2008, including 42 non-compliance actions, 8 fines, 4 probations, 4 revocations of licenses, and 41 civil or criminal prosecutions.[2]

---

[1] This does not include cases opened against applicants for licensure and individuals licensed.

[2] An official from the Oregon Mortuary and Cemetery Board clarified that the 41 civil or criminal prosecutions refers to civil actions and referrals for criminal prosecution.

Cemeteries and Cemetery Operators

Licensing requirements. In general, a person may not conduct the business of operating a cemetery without receiving a license—that is, a certificate of authority. In general, "operating cemeteries"—defined as cemeteries that (1) perform interments; (2) have fiduciary responsibilities for endowment care, general care or special care funds; or (3) have outstanding pre-need service contracts for unperformed services—must be licensed. Cemetery applicants must, among other things, pay a fee and pay biennial renewal fees. Exempt operating cemeteries—cemeteries with 10 or fewer interments annually—are not required to pay the biennial renewal fees but must maintain licensure and pay a principal fee when a new manager is assigned. A nonoperating cemetery that is not a historic cemetery—any burial place that contains the remains of one or more persons who died prior to February 14, 1909—must be registered with the Oregon Mortuary and Cemetery Board but does not need to be licensed. According to an official representing the Oregon Mortuary and Cemetery Board, there were at least 454 operating cemeteries in Oregon.

Inspection and audit requirements. The Oregon Mortuary and Cemetery Board is required to inspect licensed cemeteries every 2 years, but may conduct random inspections at other times as well.[3] In conducting inspections, the board utilizes a standard cemetery inspection checklist. According to an official representing the board, items on the checklist include whether a cemetery map, cemetery rules, and required records of internment and ownership exist. According to officials representing the Oregon Mortuary and Cemetery Board, resources are not available to do many on-site inspections. In addition, licensed cemeteries are required to keep a detailed, accurate, and permanent record of all transactions that are performed for the care and preparation and final disposition, including all remains interred or cremated and the name of the purchaser, among other information.

Consumer complaints and violations. Consumer complaints regarding cemeteries and cemetery operators are collected by various entities in Oregon. According to the state regulator who responded to our 2011 survey, the state received approximately 23 complaints against cemeteries in 2008, 15 in 2009, and 15 in 2010.[4] According to an official

---

[3] The board may not subject an exempt operating cemetery to random inspections.

[4] According to an official representing the Oregon Mortuary and Cemetery Board, this does not include cases opened against applicants for licensure and individuals licensed.

representing the Oregon Mortuary and Cemetery Board, the typical complaints received against cemeteries include failure to maintain grounds; operating without a license; failure to follow through with agreed-upon arrangements, such as markers not being installed in a timely matter; double selling a grave; inaccurate record keeping; and failing to properly supervise pre-need salespersons. Further, the state regulator who responded to this issue on our survey reported taking various enforcement actions since 2008, including 7 non-compliance actions, 2 fines, and 20 civil or criminal prosecutions. According to guidelines from the Oregon State Mortuary and Cemetery Board, with the exception of egregious or continuing violations, deficiencies noted during routine inspections rarely lead to formal disciplinary action.

Crematories and Crematory Operators

Licensing requirements. A person may not conduct the business of operating a crematory without receiving a license—that is, a certificate of authority. In 2003, the Oregon state regulator who responded to our survey provided that crematories were required to be licensed to operate in the state, but that crematory operators were not required to be licensed. Crematory applicants must, among other things, pay a fee. Certificates of authority require renewal every 2 years. According to the state regulator who responded to our 2011 survey on the regulation of crematories, there were approximately 65 crematories operating in Oregon.

Inspections and audit requirements. The Oregon Mortuary and Cemetery Board is required to inspect crematories every 2 years, but may conduct random inspections at other times as well. In conducting inspections, the board has a standard crematory inspection checklist. Items on the checklist include (1) whether the crematory license is posted and (2) whether documentation of permanent records of all transactions performed for final disposition exists. According to officials representing the Oregon Mortuary and Cemetery Board, resources are not available to do many on-site inspections.

Consumer complaints and violations. Consumer complaints regarding crematories and crematory operators are collected by various entities in Oregon. According to the state regulator who responded to our 2011 survey on the regulation of crematories, the state received approximately five complaints in 2008, two in 2009, and two in 2010. An official representing the board told us that the most frequent complaints received against crematories included failure to provide the family with the deceased's personal items and cremating without required identification tags. Officials also stated that with the increase in the cremation rate over time, there has been an increase in complaints against crematories. As a result of complaints, applications, or inspections, officials representing the Oregon Mortuary and Cemetery Board reported that they had 16 cases opened against crematories over a 3-year period—2008, 2009, and 2010.[5] Further, the state regulator who responded to this issue on our survey reported taking various enforcement actions since 2008, including two non-compliance actions, five fines, and five civil or criminal prosecutions.[6]

Cremation rate. According to the Cremation Association of North America, Oregon had a 69 percent cremation rate in 2009.[7]

Sales of Pre-Need Plans

Licensing requirements. An entity wanting to sell pre-need trusts must be certified by the Department of Consumer and Business Services (certified providers) and a salesperson employed by a certified provider must be registered with the Oregon Mortuary and Cemetery Board either as a pre-need salesperson or, among other things, licensed as a funeral service practitioner or embalmer. Individual sellers of insurance-funded pre-need plans must be insurance agents or providers, and are regulated by the Insurance Division of the Department of Consumer and Business Services.[8] A master trustee—an entity that is not a certified provider but that has fiduciary responsibility for the uniform administration of funds delivered to it by a certified provider for the benefit of purchasers of pre-need contracts—must also be registered with the Department of Consumer and Business Services. Pre-need salespersons are required to renew their registration with the Oregon Mortuary and Cemetery Board every 2 years. Submission of required annual reports and fee payments constitutes renewal of a certified provider's and master trustee's registration. According to the state regulator who responded to our 2011

---

[5] This does not include cases opened against applicants and individuals licensed.

[6] An official from the Oregon Mortuary and Cemetery Board clarified that the five civil or criminal prosecutions refers to civil penalty actions and referrals for criminal prosecutions.

[7] These data are preliminary. As of September 2011, association officials stated that the data had not been finalized.

[8] In Oregon, the sale of existing graves, crypts or niches does not constitute pre-need sales. Further, third party sellers of pre-need are exempt from licensing requirements, according to the state regulator who responded to our 2011 survey on pre-need sales.

survey on pre-need plans, there were approximately 905 salespersons and 223 companies (entities) licensed and operating in Oregon.

Inspection and audit requirements. The Department of Consumer and Business Services has the authority to audit the records of a certified provider or a master trustee.[9] In addition, certified providers and master trustees are required to file an annual report with the Department of Consumer and Business Services. According to department officials, they review these reports to identify the types of investments each master trustee is using and to ensure that certified providers have properly trusted funds they have received from consumers.

Contract and trusting requirements. Various contract and trusting requirements exist in the state of Oregon.[10]

- According to state regulators, trust-funded and insurance-funded pre-need plans are permitted in Oregon. According to the state regulator who responded to our 2011 survey, irrevocable, revocable, guaranteed, and nonguaranteed pre-need contracts are all permitted in the state but are not required.

- Each pre-need contract sold must contain certain information and disclosures. Required information or disclosures include (1) the purchaser, (2) a complete description of the goods and services purchased, (3) the master trustee or depository that will be holding the funds, and (4) identification of whether the contract is guaranteed or nonguaranteed. If the contract is guaranteed, the purchaser must disclose that they are allowed to retain 10 percent of the contract sales price. In addition, pre-need sellers are required to number each contract in consecutive order so they can be individually tracked.

- According to officials from the Department of Consumer and Business Services, certified providers must deposit pre-need funds with one of

---

[9] According to an official representing the Oregon Mortuary and Cemetery Board, for pre-need salespersons who are also licensed by the board, board inspectors review pre-need documents to ensure that only registered salespersons or licensed individuals are selling trust-funded pre-need plans at funeral homes and cemeteries. Questions of possible trusting violations are referred by the Oregon Mortuary and Cemetery Board to the Department of Consumer and Business Services.

[10] For more information on pre-need plans, see app. II.

the state's seven master trustees or in a depository (financial institution or trust company). Pre-need trust funds that are placed in a depository may only be invested in one of the following: (1) certificates of deposit; (2) U.S. Treasuries; (3) issues of U.S. government agencies; (4) guaranteed investment contracts; or (5) banker's acceptance or corporate bonds rated A or better, as specified in statute. Further, officials state that there are no limitations on the investment of pre-need trust funds placed with a master trustee.

- For guaranteed pre-need contracts, 90 percent of the amounts received for the costs of funeral and cemetery goods and services must be trusted. For nonguaranteed contracts, 100 percent of the costs of funeral and cemetery goods and services must be trusted. If a cemetery is not a certified provider, it must have a surety bond and must trust at least 66-2/3 percent of the costs of cemetery goods, such as vaults and markers that will be installed in an endowment care cemetery.

- Master trustees may pay certain fees and expenses from the earnings of the trust, limited to 2 percent of the value of the trust per year and subject to other conditions established in statute.

- According to officials from the Department of Consumer and Business Services, irrevocable trust-funded pre-need plans cannot be converted to insurance-funded pre-need plans.

- A consumer may cancel a revocable contract at any time and is entitled to receive the principal invested, plus any interest that has accrued, less any amount for service performed or merchandise delivered.

Consumer protection accounts. Oregon has a funeral and cemetery consumer protection account, which is funded from a $5 fee assessed for each pre-need contract sold. The purpose of the fund is to provide purchasers who have suffered pecuniary loss arising out of pre-need contracts with an opportunity for restitution if the provider does not have the assets or means to meet these obligations. According to officials representing the Department of Consumer and Business Services, the account was recently utilized after a small cemetery never properly trusted its funds. This was discovered when the cemetery was sold to a new owner. In November 2011, officials from the Department of Consumer and Business Services stated that to date, the fund has been used to compensate more than 160 of these purchasers for a total of over

$248,000. Further, officials stated that prior to these recent payouts, the account had just over $1.1 million in it in 2010—the maximum amount in the account since 2003.

Funds invested in pre-need trusts. Officials from the Department of Consumer and Business Services reported in November 2011 that there was approximately $108 million in pre-need funds invested through master trustees and depositories in Oregon in 2010. According to state regulators, some pre-need trust accounts have lost interest income because of the economy, but no trusts have lost principal.

Consumer complaints and violations. Consumer complaints regarding pre-need contracts are collected by various entities in Oregon. As a result of complaints or inspections, officials representing the Oregon Mortuary and Cemetery Board reported that they had 14 cases opened related to pre-need sales complaints against providers certified by the Department of Consumer and Business Services or against individual board licensees selling pre-need arrangements over a 3-year period—2008, 2009, and 2010. Further, officials from the Department of Consumer and Business Services reported in November 2011, that they identified approximately 171 violations since 2008, with the top three types of violations as follows: (1) contract funds not being trusted, (2) merchandise being listed as delivered when it was not, and (3) misrepresentation of a guaranteed versus a nonguaranteed contract.

Third Party Sellers of Funeral Goods

According to state regulators we surveyed in 2003 and 2011, other than rules or regulations that generally apply to all businesses, Oregon does not have rules or regulations in place that specifically address third party sellers of funeral goods.

Legislative Changes and Rationale

State regulatory officials we surveyed reported various changes to state laws and regulations regarding the death care industry. As reported by Oregon state regulators who responded to our 2011 surveys, changes included those that clarified legislation or regulation, enhanced consumer protections, and imposed stricter licensing requirement, and these changes either slightly or moderately strengthened the state's regulatory program. Respondents reported that these changes were a result of lobbying efforts of the death care industry and proposals from state regulatory agencies. Specific examples of these changes include provisions of laws passed in 2007 and 2009.

- A bill passed in 2007, gave the Department of Consumer and Business Services authority to (1) issue emergency orders to restrict or suspend certain certificates or registrations or to order certified providers or master trustees to cease and desist from specified conduct, and (2) to appoint a successor certified provider for a cemetery or funeral home if, among other reasons, it is appropriate to protect the interests of the purchasers and beneficiaries of pre-need contracts.

- An Oregon law passed in 2009 (1) required the licensure of death care consultants, (2) provided for the establishment of rules promoting environmentally sound death care practices, and (3) expanded the definition of cemetery. A death care consultant is defined as an individual who offers, for payment, consultations directly relating to the performance of funeral or final disposition services. Prospective death care consultant licensees are required to, among other things, pay a fee and pass an exam. Death care consultants must renew their licenses every 2 years. According to state regulators, the statutory changes regarding the environmentally sound death care practices will help position the state for future technological changes in the industry, such as alternatives methods of final disposition.[11] In addition, with the passage of this law, the definition of a cemetery was expanded to include a scattering garden or other designated area above or below ground where a person may pay to establish a memorial of cremated remains and a cenotaph where the primary purpose is to provide an area where a person may pay to establish a memorial to honor a person whose remains may be interred elsewhere or whose remains cannot be recovered.

---

[11] Alternative methods of final disposition may include such practices as alkaline hydrolysis, where a water-based chemical process is used to rapidly reduce a body to residue.

Appendix VI: Tennessee's Regulation of the Death Care Industry

Regulatory Structure

In Tennessee, two entities within the Department of Commerce and Insurance regulate the death care industry.

- The Tennessee State Board of Funeral Directors and Embalmers regulates funeral homes, funeral directors, embalmers, and crematories. The board has seven members who are appointed by the Governor—six of these members are required to be licensed funeral directors and the other member must not be affiliated with the funeral business. In addition, the board has three field representatives who inspect funeral home and crematory establishments, two administrative staff, one litigator, and one staff attorney shared with Burial Services.

- Burial Services regulates cemeteries and pre-need sales. Burial Services has four auditors who examine cemeteries and pre-need sellers, two administrative staff, and one staff attorney it shares with the Board of Funeral Directors and Embalmers.

There are no rules or regulations specific to third party sellers of funeral goods in Tennessee.

Requirements and Enforcement Mechanisms

Funeral Homes, Funeral Directors, and Embalmers

Licensing requirements. Funeral homes, funeral directors, and embalmers are required to be licensed to operate in the state, which was also was the case in 2003 as reported by the Tennessee state regulator who responded to our survey. Funeral home applicants must, among other things, pay an application fee and provide a list of all employees. Prospective funeral director and embalmer licensees must, among other things, (1) pay an application fee, (2) pass an exam, (3) complete a specified number of hours in a funeral service or mortuary sciences program, and (4) complete an apprenticeship.[1] Funeral homes, funeral

---

[1] Specifically, funeral directors are required to complete 30 semester hours in funeral service education and a 2-year apprenticeship. Embalmers are required to complete 60 semester hours in a mortuary science program and a 1-year apprenticeship.

directors, and embalmers are required to renew their licenses every 2 years. In addition, each funeral director and embalmer licensee is required to complete 10 hours of continuing education during each licensing period. According to officials representing the Tennessee Department of Commerce and Insurance, there were 562 establishments operating in Tennessee—which includes funeral homes, crematories, and embalming services.

Inspection and audit requirements. The Board of Funeral Directors and Embalmers is required to inspect funeral homes once a year. Board inspectors use a standard report form in conducting inspections, and inspect for cleanliness, documentation of licensing records, and Funeral Rule compliance, among other things. In addition, according to officials representing the Tennessee Department of Commerce and Insurance, inspectors have compared the price lists to invoices for a select number of sales to ensure that the funeral home is charging according to its price lists.[2] Officials stated that this type of comparison is not done during FTC sweeps, but told us that these types of inspections can help to uncover problems.

Consumer complaints and violations. According to officials representing the Tennessee Department of Commerce and Insurance, they received 21 complaints regarding the death care industry in 2008, 30 in 2009, and 54 in 2010, but they did not break this information down by industry segment. According to officials, the most common violations they encounter during inspections are (1) overcharging, (2) improper wording, or (3) direct cremation sales that were also charged basic service fees. Officials further stated that since 2008, they have taken 210 disciplinary actions against the segments they regulate.

Cemeteries and Cemetery Operators

Licensing requirements. Cemeteries are required to register to operate in the state unless they are otherwise exempt. The following cemeteries are exempt: (1) cemeteries owned by municipalities; (2) cemeteries owned by churches, associations of churches, or church governing bodies; (3) cemeteries owned by religious organizations; (4) family burial grounds; and (5) cemeteries owned by general welfare corporations.

---

[2] Officials stated that funeral homes may change their price lists but are required to keep records of prior price lists for a period of 1 year after its last use so that they can accurately compare price lists with sales made.

Cemetery applicants are required, among other things, to (1) pay a filing fee and (2) show proof of a cemetery map showing all interment sites. Cemeteries are required to renew their licenses every year. Officials representing the Department of Commerce and Insurance told us that Tennessee tried to pattern many of its cemetery rules after the FTC's Funeral Rule in an effort to level the playing field for the funeral home and cemetery segments of the death care industry.

Inspection and audit requirements. The Commissioner of the Department of Commerce and Insurance is responsible for auditing cemetery records at least once every 2 years. In addition, cemeteries are required to keep record of (1) every burial that shows the date, name, and location and (2) every interment site or right sold. All cemeteries that apply for a new registration after 2007 must develop and maintain a cemetery map that shows the location of sites for interment.

Consumer complaints and violations. According to officials representing the Tennessee Department of Commerce and Insurance, they received 21 complaints regarding the death care industry in 2008, 30 in 2009, and 54 in 2010, but they did not break this information down by industry segment.

Crematories and Crematory Operators

Licensing requirements. A crematory may not operate until it has been issued a license as a funeral establishment. This was also the case in 2003, as reported by the state regulator who responded to our survey. Crematory operators do not have to be licensed, but according to officials representing the Tennessee Department of Commerce and Insurance, crematories must employ at least one full-time licensed funeral director who manages the crematory. Crematory applicants are required to, among other things, pay an application fee and provide a list of all employees. Crematories are required to renew their licenses every 2 years. According to officials representing the Tennessee Department of Commerce and Insurance, there were 43 crematories operating in Tennessee.

Inspections and audit requirements. The Board of Funeral Directors and Embalmers is required to inspect crematories once a year. Board inspectors use a standard report form in conducting their inspections. The form includes items such as whether cremation records are acceptable.

Consumer complaints and violations. According to officials representing the Tennessee Department of Commerce and Insurance, they received 21 complaints regarding the death care industry in 2008, 30 in 2009, and 54 in 2010, but they did not break this information down by industry segment. Officials told us that the most common violations they see during inspections are (1) overcharging, (2) improper wording, or (3) direct cremation sales that were also charged basic service fees. Officials further stated that since 2008, they have taken 210 disciplinary actions against the segments they regulate.

Cremation rate. According to the Cremation Association of North America, Tennessee had a 23 percent cremation rate in 2009.[3]

Sales of Pre-Need Plans

Licensing requirements. Sellers of pre-need plans are required to be registered to operate in the state. To register, sellers must complete an application and pay a fee. Pre-need sellers are required to renew their registration every 2 years. According to officials representing the Tennessee Department of Commerce and Insurance, there were 495 pre-need sellers operating in Tennessee.

Inspection and audit requirements. According to an official representing the Department of Commerce and Insurance, the Commissioner of the Department of Commerce and Insurance must conduct annual examinations of pre-need sellers to ensure that each seller will be able to perform its contract with the consumer. The commissioner may also investigate or examine the affairs of any pre-need seller whenever it is deemed appropriate. In addition, every pre-need seller is required to keep and maintain, at a minimum, accurate accounts, books, and records of all pre-need contracts and insurance policy transactions. A trustee is required to keep records of, among other things, the receipt of funds and all disbursements. Pre-need sellers and trustees are required to file an annual report with the commissioner that includes a summary of the information contained in the accounts, books, and records.

Contract and trusting requirements. Various contract and trusting requirements exist in the state of Tennessee.[4]

---

[3] These data are preliminary. As of September 2011, association officials stated that the data had not been finalized.

[4] For more information on pre-need plans, see app. II.

- Trust-funded, insurance-funded, revocable, irrevocable, guaranteed, and nonguaranteed pre-need funeral plan contracts are all permitted in Tennessee.

- Prior to its use, each pre-need contract sold must contain certain information and disclosures. Required information or disclosures include (1) a statement as to whether the contract establishes a revocable trust account or an irrevocable trust account, (2) a complete disclosure of the pricing arrangement and of any contingent liabilities or costs of the buyer, and (3) a disclosure that the trustee will pay any balance remaining in the trust fund after payment for the funeral merchandise and services in accordance with the pre-need contract. Pre-need contracts must be filed with and approved by the Commissioner of the Department of Commerce and Insurance.

- Pre-need sellers are required to trust 100 percent of the sale of funeral goods and services and 120 percent of the cost of cemetery goods. A trustee is required to invest at least 50 percent of the moneys paid and placed in a pre-need funeral contract trust in the following: (1) demand deposits, (2) savings accounts, (3) certificates of deposits, or (4) other accounts issued by financial institutions.

- A trustee cannot withdraw the funds for any purpose other than payment for merchandise or service. However, the trustee can use income from the trust account to pay applicable taxes and reasonable expenses related to the administration of the trust.

- Funds deposited in trust under a pre-need funeral contract may, with the written permission of the consumer and written approval of the commissioner, be withdrawn by the trustee and used to purchase an insurance policy.

- Any funds left over in a trust after services are provided are required to be refunded to the purchaser, the purchaser's estate or otherwise named beneficiary.

Consumer protection accounts. A cemetery consumer protection account and a pre-need funeral consumer protection account exist in Tennessee. According to officials representing the Tennessee Department of Commerce and Insurance, both accounts are funded through a $20 fee assessed on each pre-need contract. Officials explained that for both accounts, half of the funds that are collected are used to support the general operation and expenses for Burial Services and the other half of the funds are used to support any receivership action initiated by the commissioner against a pre-need seller or cemetery in accordance with applicable law. Officials further stated that neither account is used to directly reimburse a consumer whose seller or trustee lost the funds the consumer contributed to a pre-need plan. According to a Tennessee industry association, there should be a true consumer protection account where the funds are set aside for consumer restitution purposes only.

Funds invested in pre-need trusts. Tennessee did not provide information on whether the state tracked the amount of funds invested in pre-need plans.

Consumer complaints and violations. According to officials representing the Tennessee Department of Commerce and Insurance, they received 21 complaints regarding the death care industry in 2008, 30 in 2009, and 54 in 2010, but they did not break this information down by industry segment.

Third Party Sellers of Funeral Goods

According to state regulators we surveyed in 2003 and 2011, other than rules or regulations that generally apply to all businesses, Tennessee does not have rules or regulations in place that specifically address third party sellers of funeral goods.[5]

Although there are no specific rules or regulations, third party sellers are subject to other state laws. In January 2010, a Tennessee court permanently enjoined the defendant from engaging in the sale of cemetery goods and services and revoked any licenses he possessed to engage in the cemetery goods and services business in the state because of his "persistent and knowing violations of the Tennessee Consumer Protection Act." The defendant was an Internet seller of cemetery goods who had failed to deliver items sold to consumers. Although the exact number of consumers affected and the total dollar amount is unknown, the final judgment of the court indicates that consumers had made 126 complaints to various agencies. The final judgment also concluded that the defendant had made at least 3,600 violations of the Tennessee Consumer Protection Act. The final judgment

---

[5] The state regulator who responded to our survey on third party sellers of funeral goods noted that third party sellers of pre-need plans were regulated.

provided that the state may seek restitution on behalf of consumers and other persons for ascertainable losses.

Legislative Changes and Rationale

Various changes to Tennessee's state laws regarding the death care industry have been made since 2003. According to officials representing the Tennessee Department of Commerce and Insurance, Tennessee enacted major revisions of funeral, cemetery, and pre-need laws and regulations in 2007 and 2008. Officials stated that these rewrites were in reaction to a pre-need incident in their state, but that in rewriting their laws, they also tried to be pro-active and address any other issues that could arise. The pre-need incident case involved the looting of about $20 million from pre-need trusts in Tennessee (see more on this incident in app. II). Changes included

- requiring state or commissioner approval for a (1) change in trustee, (2) cemetery sale, and (3) pre-need contract; and
- creating a cemetery consumer protection account and a pre-need consumer protection account.

In addition, other changes have gone into effect in Tennessee since 2003.

- All funeral establishments selling agreements, contracts, or plans for pre-need funeral services, including those that are funded through insurance, must be registered with the Commissioner of the Department of Commerce and Insurance and be subject to an annual audit.

- Cemeteries must maintain a cemetery map detailing the location of interment sites.

- Cemetery operators must make all reasonable efforts to notify known family or next of kin of a deceased individual if the operator has knowledge that the human remains of the deceased were placed in the wrong burial site.

Appendix VII: Wisconsin's Regulation of the Death Care Industry

Regulatory Structure

In Wisconsin, the Department of Regulation and Licensing regulates all segments of the death care industry. Within the department, there is a Funeral Directors Examining Board and a Cemetery Board that help regulate the funeral, cemetery, and the pre-need segments. The Funeral Directors Examining Board and the Cemetery Board both have six member positions, two of which are required to be consumer representatives. The department has 4 staff, in addition to 14 staff from the department's enforcement office who work on death care issues. However, these staff have other responsibilities and are not solely dedicated to death care issues.

In Wisconsin, cemeteries are prohibited from being affiliated with funeral homes.

Requirements and Enforcement Mechanisms

Funeral Homes, Funeral Directors, and Embalmers

Licensing requirements. Funeral directors and embalmers are required to be licensed to operate in the state, which was also was the case in 2003 as reported by the Wisconsin state regulator who responded to our survey. Funeral homes must obtain a permit to operate in the state. Prospective funeral director or embalmer licensees are required, among other things, to (1) pay an application fee, (2) complete 2 academic years of instruction in a recognized college or university, (3) complete 9 months or more of instruction in mortuary science, (4) complete a 1-year apprenticeship, and (5) pass an exam. Funeral directors and embalmers are required to renew their licenses every 2 years. Each licensee must complete 15 hours of approved continuing education during each licensing period. According to a state regulator, in November 2011 there were 514 funeral homes operating in Wisconsin.[1]

Inspection and audit requirements. According to the state regulator who responded to our 2011 survey, funeral homes are inspected if the

---

[1] Officials reported that the higher number of funeral homes reported in their survey responses likely included funeral homes that were no longer operating.

state receives a complaint. According to an official representing a Wisconsin consumer association, the state does little to monitor the industry.

Consumer complaints and violations. According to the state regulator who responded to our 2011 survey on the regulation of funeral homes, the state received approximately 81 consumer complaints in 2008, 72 in 2009, and 48 in 2010. Based on data from the Department of Regulation and Licensing, complaints included those related to (1) licensing issues, such as unlicensed practices; (2) unprofessional conduct; and (3) pricing issues, such as being charged an incorrect amount. The state regulator also reported that there were 314 violations since 2008 and that the state issued various enforcement actions that included 13 letters of reprimand, 2 fines, 7 probations, 3 relinquishments, 3 suspensions of licenses, and 2 revocations of licenses.

Cemeteries and Cemetery Operators

Licensing requirements. Cemeteries are not required to be licensed, but some cemetery operators are required to be registered or licensed to operate in the state. In 2003, as reported by the Wisconsin state regulator who responded to our survey, cemeteries were also not required to be licensed but cemetery operators had to be licensed. Specifically, a cemetery operator who (1) operates a cemetery that is 5 acres or more in size, (2) sells 20 or more cemetery lots or mausoleum spaces during a calendar year or (2) has $100,000 or more in trust fund accounts is required to be licensed. A cemetery operator that (1) operates a cemetery that is less than 5 acres in size, (2) sells fewer than 20 cemetery lots or mausoleum spaces during a calendar year, or (2) has less than $100,000 in trust fund accounts for a cemetery is required to be registered. However, a cemetery operator of a cemetery organized, maintained, and operated by any of the following are exempt from registration or licensing requirements: a town; village; city; church; synagogue or mosque; religious, fraternal or benevolent society; or incorporated college of a religious order. Prospective cemetery operator applicants must pay an application fee for licensing or registration. Licensed or registered cemetery operators are required to renew their licenses every 2 years. According to the state regulator who responded to our 2011 survey on the regulation of cemeteries, there were approximately 480 cemeteries subject to regulation operating in Wisconsin. Officials representing the Wisconsin Department of Regulation and Licensing further stated that the total number of cemeteries in the state is not known, but that the ones that are required to be licensed perform about 60 to 70 percent of all services in the state.

Inspection and audit requirements. The Department of Regulation and Licensing has the authority to inspect or audit cemeteries and cemetery authority records, among others, and may do so randomly. According to the state regulator who responded to our 2011 survey, inspections are done when the applicant for licensing first applies and when the state receives a complaint. Licensed or registered cemetery operators are required to submit an annual report to the Department of Regulation and Licensing.[2] In addition, cemeteries are required to provide price lists to consumers.

Consumer complaints and violations. According to the state regulator who responded to our 2011 survey on the regulation of cemeteries, the state received approximately 10 consumer complaints in 2008, 15 in 2009, and 3 in 2010. Based on data from the Department of Regulation and Licensing, during this time complaints included those related to (1) price issues, such as overcharging; (2) maintenance concerns; and (3) monument issues, such as placing the incorrect date on a monument. Further, according to the state regulator who responded to our 2011 survey, since 2008, there were approximately 56 violations and that the state took various enforcement actions, including one letter of reprimand, two assessments of investigative costs, one relinquishment of a license, and one revocation of a license.

Crematories and Crematory Operators

Licensing requirements. Crematory operators are required to register to operate in the state. There are no requirements that a crematory be registered or licensed. To apply for registration, crematory operators are required, among other things, to (1) pay an application fee and (2) provide, among other things, a description of the equipment that will be used. Crematory operators are required to renew their registrations every 2 years. According to the state regulator who responded to our 2011 survey, there were approximately 98 crematories operating in the state.

Inspections and audit requirements. According to the state regulator who responded to our 2011 survey, inspections are done if there is a complaint filed with the Department of Regulation and Licensing. In

---

[2] Although not regulated, religious cemeteries may file annual certifications declaring that they have followed state statute.

addition, a crematory operator is required to keep records of each
cremation performed.

Consumer complaints and violations. According to the state regulator
who responded to our 2011 survey on the regulation of crematories, the
state received approximately one consumer complaint in 2008, none in
2009, and three in 2010. Based on data from the department, complaints
received from 2007 through March 2011 included those related to
(1) environmental concerns, such as black smoke being emitted from the
facility, and (2) not obtaining proper authorization for cremation. Further,
according to the state regulator who responded to our survey, since 2008,
there were approximately 16 violations, with the most common violation
being related to fraud or deceptive practices.

Cremation rate. According to the Cremation Association of North
America, Wisconsin had a 42 percent cremation rate in 2009.[3]

Sales of Pre-Need Plans

Licensing requirements. Sellers of pre-need plans are required to be
licensed to operate in the state, which was also the case in 2003 as
reported by the Wisconsin state regulator who responded to our survey.
Sellers of pre-need plans must renew their licenses every 2 years.

Inspection and audit requirements. Pre-need sellers may be required
to file an annual report, which is to include accounting of all amounts
deposited and withdrawn from pre-need accounts. The Department of
Regulation and Licensing is required to review such reports.

Contract and trusting requirements. Various contract and trusting
requirements exist in the state of Wisconsin.[4]

- Trust-funded, insurance-funded, revocable, irrevocable, guaranteed,
  and nonguaranteed pre-need funeral plan contracts are all permitted
  in Wisconsin. According to officials representing the Wisconsin
  Department of Regulation and Licensing, insurance-funded plans are

---

[3] These data are preliminary. As of September 2011, association officials stated that the
data had not been finalized.

[4] For more information on pre-need plans, see app. II.

more common in the funeral segment and trust-funded plans are more common in the cemetery segment of the industry.

- Pre-need sellers are required to trust either an amount equal to at least 40 percent of each payment of principal that is received from the sale of cemetery merchandise under a pre-need sales contract into a pre-need trust fund, or the wholesale cost ratio for the cemetery merchandise multiplied by the amount of the payment of principal that is received, whichever is greater. For the pre-need sale of funeral goods and services, 100 percent of funds must be trusted with either a bank or trust company within the state whose deposits are insured by the Federal Deposit Insurance Corporation, deposited in a savings and loan association or savings bank within the state whose deposits are insured by the Federal Deposit Insurance Corporation, or invested in a credit union within the state whose savings are insured by the national board.

- For the pre-need sale of funeral goods or services, funds must remain in trust, including interest and dividends, if any, until the death of the potential decedent, unless they are released upon demand to the depositor (the purchaser of the pre-need goods or services) after written notice is provided to the beneficiary (the pre-need seller).

- A request by a cemetery authority to transfer funds to a different trustee must be approved by the Department of Regulation and Licensing.

Consumer protection accounts. According to the Wisconsin state regulator who responded to our survey, no consumer protection fund exists in Wisconsin.

Funds invested in pre-need trusts. According to the state regulator who responded to our survey, Wisconsin tracks the amount of money invested in pre-need plans. Wisconsin did not provide data on the amount of money currently invested in these plans.

Consumer complaints and violations. Officials representing the Department of Regulation and Licensing told us that they receive few complaints.

Third Party Sellers of Funeral Goods

Third party sales are subject to some degree of regulation, but sellers are not required to be licensed to operate in the state.

Legislative Changes and Rationale

The state regulatory official we surveyed reported various changes to state laws and regulations regarding the death care industry. As reported by the Wisconsin state regulator who responded to our 2011 surveys, changes included those that imposed stricter licensing requirements and enhanced consumer protections, and these changes moderately strengthened the state's regulatory program. The state regulator who responded to our survey reported that these changes were a result of proposals from state agencies. Changes included the following bills that were passed.

- The Cemetery Registration & Consumer Protection Act, passed in 2007, brought more cemeteries under regulation. According to officials representing the Wisconsin Department of Regulation and Licensing, under this act, about 1,200 to 1,500 cemeteries now fall under registration or licensing requirements. Officials compared this to 1991, when only 5 cemeteries were required to be licensed. Officials also stated that the genesis for the legislative expansion was a general recognition by the state legislature that it was appropriate to have more oversight of cemeteries and that the effort to pass the law was spearheaded by a Wisconsin industry association.

- Assembly Bill 485, passed in 2006, required that except for performing funeral services, the business of a funeral director must be conducted in a funeral establishment that has been issued a permit by the examining board.

- Assembly Bill 75, passed in 2006, created the Crematory Authority Council and required that crematory authorities be registered.

- Assembly Bill 100, passed in 2005, created the Cemetery Board as an oversight mechanism for cemeteries.

Appendix VIII: GAO Contact and Staff Acknowledgments

GAO Contact	William O. Jenkins, Jr., (202) 512-8777 or jenkinswo@gao.gov
Staff Acknowledgments	In addition to the contact named above, John Mortin, Assistant Director; Tracey Cross; Dorian Dunbar; Stuart Kaufman; Thomas Lombardi; Jessica Orr; Minette Richardson; and Greg Wilmoth made significant contributions to this report.